CHRISTMAS COLLECTABLES

DEDICATION

To my dearest darling Aunty Lilly, whose
fond childhood memories of family Christmas parties
will always stay with me, as will you in my heart.

CHRISTMAS COLLECTABLES

by

TRACY MARTIN

with a foreword by

CHRISTOPHER BIGGINS

REMEMBER WHEN

First published in Great Britain in 2009 by
REMEMBER WHEN
An imprint of
Pen & Sword Books Ltd
47 Church Street
Barnsley
South Yorkshire
S70 2AS

ISBN 978 1 84468 064 1

Typeset by Phoenix Typesetting, Auldgirth, Dumfriesshire
Printed and bound by Kyodo Nation Printing Services

Pen & Sword Books Ltd incorporates the Imprints of Pen & Sword Aviation,
Pen & Sword Maritime, Pen & Sword Military, Wharncliffe Local History,
Pen & Sword Select, Pen & Sword Military Classics,
Leo Cooper, Remember When, Seaforth Publishing and Frontline Publishing.

For a complete list of Pen & Sword titles please contact
PEN & SWORD BOOKS LIMITED
47 Church Street, Barnsley, South Yorkshire, S70 2AS, England
E-mail: enquiries@pen-and-sword.co.uk
Website: www.pen-and-sword.co.uk

CONTENTS

FOREWORD

BY CHRISTOPHER BIGGINS

My most vivid childhood Christmas memory is hanging up the stocking in the hope that Father Christmas would fill it full of lovely gifts. Like most children I also placed a glass of sherry and some biscuits on the mantelpiece as a treat for when Santa arrived with his reindeers. In the morning to my delight the sherry had gone and there were just a few crumbs left of the biscuit but even more exciting was the bulging stocking full of presents.

Today I still adore Christmas, although much of mine is usually spent appearing in one of the pantomime shows that traditionally run throughout the Christmas season around the country, so I only get one day off – Christmas Day.

This I spend with my godchildren in Oxford and we have a traditional Christmas day participating in the ritual of opening presents, eating turkey and just enjoying the festivities.

Then it is back to work for me until the middle of January. The pantomime is an integral part of the Christmas celebrations which dates back to the Middle Ages and I have played many characters over the years including various pantomime dames with my most favourite being the Hamlet of all pantomime dames – Mother Goose. The largest part for a dame in any pantomime show, Mother Goose as we know the story today was first played at the Drury Lane Theatre in London in 1902 by Dan Leno a well-known comedian of the time. He performed the part as a plain old woman who longs to be young and beautiful but the moral of the story is that beauty doesn't necessarily bring happiness.

I love performing in these seasonal shows and as Christmas is all about children it is fantastic to see the little ones in the audience with happy faces contributing with the pantomime tradition of shouting, 'He's behind you,' cheering at the good characters and booing at the baddies. In fact a child's Christmas isn't complete without a trip to the theatre to see the pantomime.

When Tracy Martin told me that she was writing this book *Christmas Collectables* and asked yours truly if I would write the foreword I was delighted to accept her offer. I have known Tracy since she first appeared as a regular collectables expert on the radio show for BBC London, which I co-hosted with Lesley Joseph. Tracy is not only extremely knowledgeable in all things collectable but is also a passionate collector herself.

Like me, Tracy adores Christmas and throughout the pages of this book she has delved into the social history, traditions and collectablity of this festive season. You will certainly learn a lot as you read, I did, and if you are as passionate about Christmas as Tracy and myself then I strongly recommend that this book is top of your Christmas list when you write to Santa this year.

Christopher Biggins
Actor, Comedian, Presenter and 'The' Christmas Pantomime Dame

INTRODUCTION

Imagine an enormous Christmas tree decorated with twinkling lights, the joyous sound of carol singers trudging through the snow and a family sitting around a table laden with festive foods, all excited about pulling the home-made crackers and hoping to be the lucky person to discover the concealed sixpence in the plum pudding. Christmas – a time for celebration, goodwill to all men and an excuse for me to become overexcited and spend copious amounts of money. I absolutely adore this time of year.

The whole season is magical, and has been for me since childhood. I remember tiptoeing downstairs early Christmas morning to find presents piled high under the tree, with the smell of turkey wafting from the kitchen. The radio would blare out Christmas songs whilst my brother and I frantically tore off the festive paper on our bulging Christmas stocking gifts. Everything about the day was perfect, uncomplicated and really good fun. Even now, I still hold those nostalgic childhood memories and try to relive them in my adult life by making Christmas just as it was back then.

However, even though I love the 25th December it is the run up to the festive season which I enjoy most. The shopping for presents, decorating of the tree, constant humming of Christmas carols and writing out all those cards to send to people I probably haven't even spoken to for the last twelve months. I just can't get enough so once the festivities have come to an end I look for other ways to feed my appetite for Christmas. This usually is in the form of hunting down all those vintage and discontinued Christmas collectables. I will scour internet sites, visit collectors' centres and trawl the boot sales in order to find anything and everything associated with this time of year

So you cannot imagine how pleased I was when approached to write this *Christmas Collectables* book. An avid collector myself, the book combines two of my biggest passions – Christmas and collectables. There is so much on offer when it comes to all those festive items, from the wonderful array of Christmas tree lights to the big glass baubles that used to hang on my family Christmas tree, all of which are now highly sought after by collectors. Not forgetting, of course the extensive range of various Christmas ornaments such as the very sought after Royal Doulton and Coalport 'The Snowman' figurines which are always highly regarded in collectable circles.

Over the past ten years in my role as a collectables expert I have written many articles on Christmas. Some have been on general Christmas themes whilst others have been dedicated to a specific subject. I remember one particular piece that I wrote on a passionate snowman collector whose whole home was a shrine to this festive figure. Another of my features for a collectables magazine was on a man who decorated his entire house in Christmas memora-bilia during October so that he could open it up for the public to view in December. His collection included everything from Lladro figurines through to Christmas film posters, vintage Christmas cards to fairy lights. Even his front room was turned into Santa's grotto.

Throughout the pages of this book I will be sharing my knowledge on Christmas collect-ables, including information on what is worth collecting, where to buy and how to distinguish a modern piece from a vintage one. I will also be talking about the history behind the Christmas collectable items and why the folklores and traditions are a major contributing factor to the appeal of Christmas and the items associated with it.

With so much to choose ranging from decorations to Christmas cards and toys to ceramics this enormous collecting category crosses over into many different areas but yet all comes together to create one of the biggest and most popular – Christmas memorabilia.

A book that will not only appeal to collectors but to those that adore Christmas, I am hoping that even the Scrooges amongst us will become enticed into the festive spirit.

TRACY MARTIN

THE ORIGINS
OF CHRISTMAS

Before I actually get started on the world of Christmas collectables I think it is important to first explain the origins and traditions behind how and why we celebrate this festive season.

Today, we recognise this annual holiday as a celebration of the birth of Jesus Christ, the Son of God even though we know he wasn't actually born on this day but possibly some months earlier. However, it is has become the norm to give praise and honour to this Christian figure every 25 December.

One of the largest contributors to Christmas celebrations was the pagans and throughout the pages of this book you will see that many of our traditions around the festive season have evolved from their folklore, beliefs and customs.

The ancient city of Babylon (south of Baghdad) has also contributed to our Christmas celebrations, as each year a feast was held on 25 December in honour of the Goddess of Nature (son of Isis). At this feast was much gift giving, eating and drinking – a more or less mirror image of what families do across the world today on the same date.

Rome also contributed to seasonal celebrations as each year they would honour Saturn, the God of Agriculture, in a festival of Winter Solstice. One of the traditions during this period of celebration was to send singers and dancers adorned in costume to travel from house to house in order to entertain their neighbours. Much like the carol singers we find on our doorsteps each year during the festive season.

Across Europe (especially the Northern hemispheres) celebrations had also taken part long before Jesus stepped foot on the earth. They too had their own Winter Solstice, which was known as 'Yule' (wheel) a pagan word for sun. Logs would be burnt in honour of the Sun God, Mithra, in order to hold celebration to the fact that people were coming out of the winter season into the warmer and longer days of summer. At this time mistletoe and evergreens were considered sacred, so people would bring them into their homes during the winter months in order to keep the evergreens safe until they could be returned to the outside in the summer. It was also known as good luck as these evergreens would help people's crops grow when the summer finally did reappear. Today, much of our traditions stem from these pagan celebrations, such as the 'kissing under the mistletoe' and decorating of a Christmas tree.

However, it is said that it was the Romans who eventually turned these pagan traditions into a Christian holiday. Around the Sixth Century missionaries were sent to Britain from Rome in order to convert people to Christianity. They soon realised that people couldn't necessarily be converted overnight so suggested that the annual pagan celebrations still be held but be in honour of Christ's birth instead of the Winter Solstice. St Augustine (founder of the first church in Britain) agreed to help the missionaries convert the people to the teachings of Christ and so gradually Winter Solstice celebrations would change to a celebration of the birth of Christ.

Although there is much debate as to which church did actually initiate Christmas as being a symbolic celebration to Christ, it is pretty much obvious that right across the world various countries, religions and traditions all contributed to this day which now we know as Christmas Day, 25 December – a celebration of the birth of Jesus.

Christmas is a time to celebrate the birth of Jesus Christ, the Son of God.

CHAPTER 1

CHRISTMAS TREES

'I have been looking on; this evening at a merry company of children assembled around that pretty Germany toy, a Christmas tree'

From Charles Dickens *A Christmas Tree*, 1850.

What is the first thing that you do with regard to Christmas celebrations – I don't mean shopping for presents in September or buying your Christmas cards in the January sales – but the first real Christmassy event that you partake in? For me, it is assembling and decorating the Christmas trees (yes, I have three in total). An integral part of the festive season, the tree gets me into the seasonal mood and it is a task I take incredibly seriously as I must have it completed on 1 December. Now I realise most people aren't as keen as I am and either share this experience further on into the month with their children or wait until the panic sets in, frantically pulling decorations out of the loft because they have left it too late; but for me, this is the beginning of my Christmas. A glass of port in one hand, mince pies piled high on a plate and Christmas songs playing in the background I begin to set about the job of decorating the trees. Once finished, I stand back and admire my handiwork – Christmas has finally begun . . .

A collectable Christopher Radko Christmas tree glass ornament 'Bountiful Boughs'.

In the Seventh Century a Devonshire Monk, St Boniface was sent to Germany to convert the pagans to Christianity. Legends are conflicting but some say that he found pagans worshiping an oak tree, so in anger he cut it down and a fir grew in its place. The pagans saw this as the work of God so became Christians and worshiped the fir as 'God's Tree'. Another story is that when St Boniface found the worshipping pagans he used the shape of a fir tree to describe the Holy Trinity of God the Father, Son, and Holy Spirit and so pagans revered the fir, being God's Tree.

A German Christmas

Although today we accept that the majority of homes will have a Christmas tree decorated with everything from glass baubles to tinsel and fairy lights to sugar canes, this wasn't always the case in Britain. Originally a German tradition, many of the Germans residing in England would display their Christmas fir trees with pride in their homes but it wasn't a general trend that filtered out amongst the British people. However the wife of George III, the Hanoverian Queen Charlotte, brought one over for the festivities at the Royal Court in 1800. Unfortunately, the British people were unsettled about taking up this German Christmas tradition as they were not particularly fond of the German monarchy, so only a few people followed the fashions of the court and displayed Christmas trees in their homes.

Throughout history it has been the real fir tree that has been used as a symbol of Christmas.

Victorian Christmas

This was all to change when Queen Victoria and her new German Consort, Prince Albert, were illustrated standing around a decorated tree with their family on the front page of *The London News* in 1846. Queen Victoria was popular with the people of Britain so if she was seen to take the lead on something, then her subjects would follow. Thus the popularity of the Christmas tree began not only in England but in America as well and has stayed part of our festive celebrations ever since.

Dickensian Festivities

We also mustn't forget the major influence that the writer, Charles Dickens, had on the

Victorian Christmas. His stories often featured joyous Christmas celebratory scenes such as the Fezziwig Ball in *A Christmas Carol* and Christmas at Dingley Dell in *Pickwick Papers*, both having significant reference to that 'Germany toy, a Christmas tree'.

REAL FIR TREES

Throughout history, it is the real fir tree that has been used within the home as a symbol of Christmas. Even today this real variety is used by many, and I myself remember as a child the excitement of my dad arriving home with the tree that he had finally decided would be perfect for us. It had obviously to be the right size, with plenty of branches and not too sparse at the top so that when it was decorated it gave off the desired effect of looking well balanced and evenly decorated. Back in the 1970s/80s the trees were sold with their roots and it was an arduous task for my father to find the right-sized bucket and replant the tree in order that it would survive the festive season. I also remember my mum cursing as the pine needles would start to scatter all over the floor and she was forever hoovering. Sometimes even in February we would still find the odd pine needle embedded into the carpet. The smell is another distinctive factor of having a real tree; the pine smell would fill the lounge and jolt you back to the realisation that Christmas Day was just around the corner.

COLLECTABLE TREES

When it comes to the serious business of collecting Christmas trees, this is a tricky area to consider as the Victorians used real trees, so of course they no longer exist and pre-war trees are hard to find. Post-war trees can still be hunted out but with many collectors sourcing the few that remain this is a difficult Christmas collectable to track down. However, if you are still determined to see if you can lay your hands on one of these wonderful trees then this is what you should be looking for.

A FEATHERED HISTORY

After Queen Victoria died in January 1901, the Christmas tree seemed to loose its popularity, with very few homes still displaying one during the Yuletide festivities. Those houses that did still carry on the tradition favoured trees made of goose, turkey, swan or ostrich feathers which were dyed green to give the effect of pine. This tree was the first ever artificial tree to be invented, again originating from Germany it was a necessity as deforestation was widespread throughout Germany due to the fact that they had been lopping off the tops of the real trees for export, thus making it impossible for the rest of the tree to grow taller and was useless as a timber tree.

The first recorded date that the feather tree appeared is in 1845; it was made of metal wire or sticks which were then covered with the feathers. These sticks were then drilled into a larger one to resemble branches. There were wide spaces between the branches and the

Christmas trees were made of swan, goose, turkey and ostrich feathers which were dyed green to give the look of short pine needles and many were used to decorate the tabletop.

feathers were made to look like short pine needles as the idea was that they resembled the locally grown white pine.

The majority of the feather trees were extremely sparse and not as thick and lush as today's trees. They were also used as tabletop decorations, as most measured from as small as 17" in height up to 50".

Feather trees continued to appear in the decades that followed the Victorian era and were most popular during the 1920s. By the 1930s their popularity had started to decline as the real tree industry had grown.

During the Second World War the British looked upon their Christmas as a security blanket, an event that hasn't changed. Despite the fact that the Christmas tree was of German origin they started to use their small tabletop feather trees again as they could be easily moved to an air raid shelter. After the war had finished, Germany took up production once more and began to make the feather trees in a variety of colours, which included pink and white.

Good examples of these feathered trees are extremely hard to come by and are amongst the most highly prized Christmas collectables. I have seen early examples sell on internet auctions and prices vary depending on their age, height, condition and colour. The best examples tend to sell for around £400 whilst small ones that do not have as many feathers left on the branches can sell for around the £100 mark. Replica feather trees are also being made now, some of which are fantastically executed and produced in the exact style as the vintage varieties. However, some of the modern manufacturers are not quite as well made so please make sure when buying you know exactly what you are getting. It can be difficult to tell the difference between a modern and an original vintage Christmas tree but here are some pointers, which will hopefully help you.

How Spot a Modern Feather Tree

- The modern examples are not as flimsy as the vintage trees.
- They have a more durable, sturdy base.
- The branches are made with thicker wire to hold heavier ornaments.
- There are more feathers on each branch so the tree is not as sparse.
- The bottom branches are wider giving a more natural tree look as opposed to the vintage trees which still have sparse thinner branches at the bottom as well as the top.

After the war Germany once again began to produce feather trees but this time in a variety of colours including pink.

FROM TOILET BRUSH TO CHRISTMAS TREES

Even though the feather tree was the very first artificial tree, you might be surprised to know that the first artificial brush tree was invented by a company that manufactured toilet brushes. Yes, it's true – the American Addis Brush Company came up with the idea during the 1930s and used the same machinery that manufactured the toilet bowl brush. In fact quite a few manufacturers started to progress their businesses this way. Royal Doulton were originally sanitaryware manufacturers before turning their hands to ceramics and Airfix made toothbrushes.

The new artificial brush tree by Addis had a strong advantage over the feather tree as it was able to support the weight of heavier decorations. Their famous 'Silver-Pine' tree came along much later and was patented in 1950. Made of aluminium the branches shot upwards rather than outwards and were very modernistic in design. Another revolutionary factor to

*White feather trees were
also a popular colour in
the home during the
1930s.*

the 'Silver-Pine' was that it had a revolving light source underneath which meant that light shone in different colours as it revolved around the base of the tree. This light source meant that the tree could stand alone without fairy lights or even decorations if the owner felt the need wasn't necessary. Popularity for this particular artificial tree really took off in the 1960s and it was found in many homes across Britain and America.

From a collecting point of view these trees are very hard to find, especially the earlier models from the 1930s, so command a premium if discovered.

EVERGLEAM

In 1959 the very first all aluminium tree was introduced to the public. Manufactured by The Aluminium Speciality Company their Sales Manager, Tom Gannon, came to them with the idea a year earlier. The 'Evergleam' became their flagship tree, although was advertised as a permanent tree rather than an artificial one. Easy to assemble, it was similar in look to the 'Silver-Pine'. It had a silver painted wooden trunk and the branches perched upwards to resemble the shape of a traditional tree and it was held up with an aluminium tripod stand, which again had a wheel of colour around the base. The downfall of this particular Christmas tree was in fact due to a television cartoon *Peanuts* starring the character Charlie Brown. In the cartoon Charlie was looking for a Christmas tree but refused to buy one of the aluminium trees even if it was the popular pink one. This caused the companies to stop producing the aluminium trees as people began to say it was crass commercialisation. Now collectors will pay a premium to own the aluminium trees especially if in different colours. Quite hard to track down it is normally the silver example which is easiest to find and depending on condition can sell from as little as £50 up to £150, sometimes even just the coloured wheel alone can fetch around £60. The most sought after and hardest colour to find is pink and if you manage to find one in really good condition this could sell for as much as £300 upwards.

Christmas Today

The Victoria and Albert Museum in London has commissioned famous fashion designers, in recent years, to design the Christmas tree that stands in their grand entrance. Jasper Conran, Matthew Williamson, Alexander McQueen and Tord Boontje have designed recent trees.

The artificial trees of today are extremely realistic and come in all shapes and sizes. You can choose between more traditional ones with pine cones to white trees and even black was a fashion must-have a few years ago. Everyone has different tastes for their own Christmas. I personally have a more traditional 6ft green artificial tree in my lounge and in the other sitting area a smaller 5ft silver artificial one. Outside the house I decorate a real fir tree, which is a welcoming sight for any visitors or passers-by. There is no real rulebook for the modern Christmas tree – it is simply buy whatever you like. Some prefer real fir as nothing beats the look and smell of a pine tree whilst others like the fibre-optic designs and I, personally, love my artificial ones. I am convinced that my retro-looking silver tree is guaranteed to be collect-able at some point in the future, especially if I keep the original packing.

INTERESTING CHRISTMAS TREE FACTS
- A fir tree hung with apples was used as a prop in a popular German medieval play about Adam and Eve. It was named 'The paradise tree' as it represented the Garden of Eden.
- The Christmas tree is said to have evolved from pagan tradition

as people would often decorate trees and evergreens as a symbol of their gods.

- The ancient Romans used to decorate trees with small pieces of metal during their winter festival, Saturnalia – which was in celebration of Saturnus, the God of Agriculture. They also exchanged evergreen branches as good luck.

A wonderful vintage tabletop Christmas tree with stunning Christmas winter village scene at the base.

- The Druids decorated trees with signs of prosperity such as coins for wealth, fruit for harvest, and fertility charms.
- In the Twelfth Century the fir was hung upside down from ceilings as a symbol of Christianity.
- The first printed reference to Christmas trees appeared in Germany in 1531.
- In the Sixteenth Century, one of history's most important reformers, Martin Luther, decorated a small Christmas tree with candles, to show his children how the stars twinkled at night.
- Every year since 1947 the people of Oslo, Norway, have given a Christmas tree to England. The gift is an expression of goodwill and gratitude for Britain's help to Norway during World War Two and is erected in Trafalgar Square.
- The 26th President of the United States, Teddy Roosevelt, banned the Christmas tree from the White House (and his home) for environmental reasons during his time in office (1901-1909).
- In 1963, the National American Christmas Tree was not lit until December 22nd because there was a thirty-day mourning following the assassination of President Kennedy on 22nd November 1963.

CHAPTER 2

FAIRY LIGHTS TO BUBBLE DELIGHTS

The tree stood proud ablaze with light, for every light was burning bright.

From the *Gospel Tree*, Anonymous

Let's be honest, a Christmas tree looks pretty dull until it is covered in all those wondrous coloured fairy lights and decorations. The lighting is the first thing that I tackle as once these are on they bring the tree alive in all its festive glory. I tend to use coloured fairy lights for the traditional tree and blue sparkling ones for the silver tree. Then outside on my real fir I use either white lights, or if feeling really adventurous, lots of purple ones around the branches. I don't just stop at the trees either, I place lights all over the house, winding them around the staircase, hanging them in the windows and of course I have to make sure the outside of the house is blazoned with colour. However we are all aware how this can be the biggest chore when it comes to the Christmas preparations: are all the lights working? Do replacement bulbs need to be bought? Not, forgetting the arduous task of unravelling the lights as they were just cast aside into a box last January.

So where did the Christmas lights originate: who came up with the idea of placing them on the tree, and which ones are the must-have collectable lights that we all crave today?

TWINKLING LIGHTS

Let's start at the very beginning. A tradition that dates back to the Middle Ages, people originally used real candles to decorate their Christmas tree. The idea was that the candles would illuminate the other decorations which hung on the tree by being strategically placed onto the branches. The candles were originally applied with melted wax then secured in place with pins. During the Victorian era another way of displaying the candles was by placing them in holders, which were known as illumination lamps. These holders were made of glass and resembled a pineapple shape. The candle would sit snugly inside the glass lamp which was hooked with wire onto the branches of the tree. The actual glass lamps had a diamond design on the outside so that when the lit candle shone through it reflected what

Before Fairy lights came into existence people would use real burning candles on their trees which were strategically placed onto the branches.

looked like fairy wings – hence the name fairy lights was born.

Available in an assortment of colours from clear glass to cobalt blue, purple to cranberry, one of the rarer colours to find is that of a deep raspberry. However the rarest of all the Victorian Christmas lamps is a 'Barth's' as it was not particularly successful in its day. These lamps held a liquid which was burnt with a wick. Usually if found, these rare lamps carry the embossed mark on the bottom of the glass with a date and they are even more scarce with the original shade attached. Highly sought after by collectors they rarely come onto the market.

> In the Sixteenth Century, a German Monk, church reformer, and father of Protestantism named Martin Luther, decorated his Christmas tree with candles in order to show his children how the stars twinkled at night.

BRIGHT LIGHT

Of course there was the dangerous issue of a fire hazard with real candles sitting on a tree and I dread to think how many people's homes went up in smoke during the festive

Illumination lamps were popular in the Victorian era, made of glass the candle would sit snugly inside.

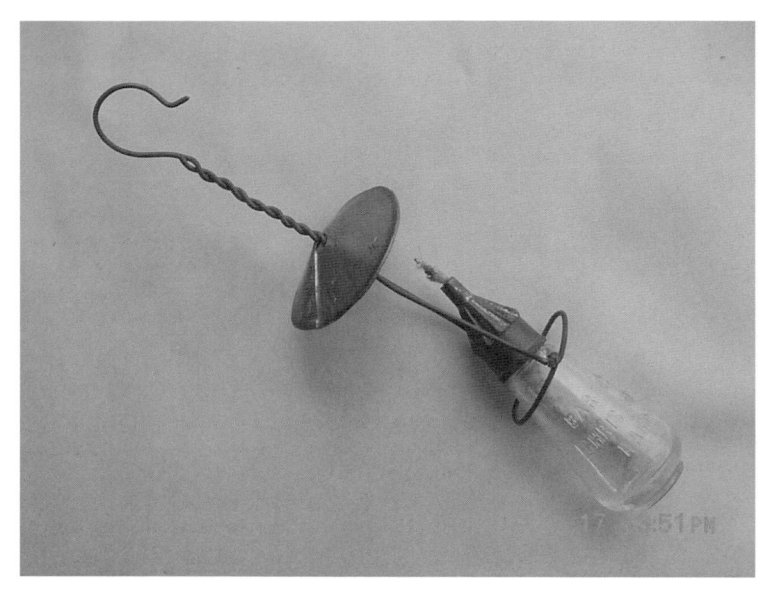

The rare Victorian 'Barth's Lamp' held a liquid which was burnt with a wick.

period. I even remember my friend telling me that her mum would keep a bucket of water nearby – just in case one of the candles toppled over . . .

So it was inevitable that someone would come up with a safer option. It was Edward Johnson, an assistant to the inventor Thomas Edison (well-known for inventing his version of the practical light bulb) who in 1882 discovered that a Christmas tree could be lit with electricity. His first attempt was on his own tree at his home in New York which he decorated with eighty small bulbs. Realising this worked, Edward went on to mass-produced strings of Christmas tree lights, which by the 1900s were appearing within department stores as part of their Christmas shop window displays. However, the common person continued to use candles to decorate their tree as these new electric Christmas lights were just too expensive to buy. It wasn't until a few decades later in the 1930s that electrical Christmas lights became popular and part of everyone's Christmas celebrations.

The earliest known advertisement for Christmas tree lamps appeared on the 28th November 1900 in the Scientific American Magazine. This advert offered to sell or rent Christmas lights.

SAFETY FIRST

The other issue with the new lights was that they still weren't particularly safe and still possessed the issue of a potential fire hazard if they became too hot. This was to be rectified in 1917 by a fifteen-year-old boy named Albert Saddaca. By adapting the novelty lighting that his parents produced he was able to create electrical safety lights which could be used on trees as well as general decoration. The first year of production saw just 100 strings of white lights sell but the second year Saddaca concentrated on producing multi-coloured ones. These proved a huge success and resulted in the company taking off. Some years later Saddaca together with his two brothers, Henri and Leon, set up NOMA Electricity and proceeded to corner the Christmas light market right through until the 1960s.

A QUALITY TRADEMARK – MAZDA

Some people might be mistaken to believe that Mazda is a manufacturing name for Christmas lights, but this is not so. Taking its name from 'Ahura Mazda – the God of Light' it was actually a trademark. American company General Electric were the first to use the Mazda name on their lights in 1909 and this trademark continued to be a sign to the worldwide public of quality, long life and the best in lighting that they could buy. So when you see those famous Mazda Mickey Mouse lights dating to around the 1930s remember they are actually manufactured by The British Thomson-Houston Company Ltd and not made by the company named Mazda.

COLLECTABLE DELIGHTS

Today, vintage tree lights are amongst one of the most highly collected of Christmas decorations – although they can be relatively hard to come by.

There are many who choose to collect lights dating from the Victorian era right up until present day. Whilst others tend to concentrate on the very early examples, others prefer lights dating from the 1960s and 1970s, and there are those collectors who prefer to collect lights that have a novelty element attached. Many collectors look to certain manufacturers but probably the biggest defining factor for Christmas light collecting is the actual materials that they are made from. The very early lights were created in Germany and were made from clear glass. These early examples are prized possessions with collectors as few survived, many being broken over the years. In later years other forms of material such as heavy-duty fire resistant plastics appeared. A vast and interesting collecting area there is far more to simple Christmas lights than you might think, not only does each have an in-depth history, but there are also many varieties to consider.

GERMAN CLEAR GLASS LIGHTS

Although the Americans invented the Christmas light it wasn't long before other countries jumped on the bandwagon. Germany, being the originator of many of our most popular Christmas traditions such as the Christmas tree, also began to produce lights. Made from clear glass they were incredibly detailed and production for these lights remained in Germany right up until the First World War when Japan took over the industry.

Three very early German clear glass painted lights having exhaust tip points.

POST-WAR LIGHTS

By the end of the First World War milk glass (an opaque glass which has the appearance of porcelain) had been invented and the majority of lights were being made from this glass by machine in Japan. Production costs were cheap so they were able to offer huge quantities of them. Although initially not as detailed or the same standard as the original German clear glass lights it wasn't long before the Japanese figural lights dominated the industry.

The appeal of milk glass was that it adhered well to being painted with colours, also that should the paint flake it left an attractive opalescent glass colour peeping through, rather than just clear glass. To start with the Japanese lights were very crude but over time they became more detailed and nicely painted. However by the end of the Second World War the Japanese lighting industry had died due to the introduction of more sophisticated Christmas tree lighting.

Milk glass lights appealed to people as when the paint flecked off it left an attractive opalescent glass colour peeping through rather than just clear glass.

Milk glass tree lights are extremely sought after by collectors, especially the early examples. You can determine an original old milk glass one to a later more modern one by holding it up to the light. A Christmas light that has some age will appear almost translucent, as if you are looking through it, the edges are also a good indication of old milk glass as this is where it is the thinnest. Condition is also really important. Due to the lights being painted onto glass the ones that do exist can suffer with paint flecks missing. The price can be affected depending on how much of the paint has come off. There is also the subject matter to consider, these particular glass lights were made in various guises from animals and birds, through to Chinese lanterns and Christmas figures – I have even seen an American Zeppelin before. You can still track these milk glass decorations down through internet auctions and specialist Christmas collecting sites, although with all Christmas collectables Americans are the most avid enthusiasts, so you tend to get the best examples and the best deals if you are prepared to buy from America.

Shown here are two early Humpty Dumpty lights, the one on the left is a German clear glass painted light whilst the one on the right is an early milk glass Japanese copy.

BUBBLE LIGHTS

Another breakthrough in Christmas lighting was the bubble light. Patented in 1935 by the inventor, Carl Otis who was working for the American company Montgomery Wards (the first ever mail order retail company) as an accountant. Otis offered his bubble lights to his employers, sadly they refused to sponsor him so Otis took his new invention to NOMA who immediately saw the potential and bought the rights. The bubble light went on to become the biggest selling light of its time in America.

If you didn't have a bubble light on your Christmas tree by the late 1940s then you were a Christmas outcast. This was the light to own and there were many to choose from. The first set of 'Bubble Lites' were available from NOMA in 1946, packaged in a book-style box. The first light to go on sale was the NOMA Biscuit and was continually sold in variations up until the company went into bankruptcy in 1965.

The lights themselves were glass tubes filled with the chemical methylene chloride. They had a plastic base which held the bulb in contact with the tube. The light would then 'bubble' away when heated. In fact they had such a low boiling point that even the heat from hands would ensure bubbling. As with anything that proves a success other companies wanted a piece of the action and this is what happened with the NOMA 'Bubble Lites' – suddenly by 1947 everyone was marketing their own style of bubble lighting.

THEY BUBBLE! THEY SPARKLE!

The liquid inside the first set of lights produced by NOMA was tinted different colours and this is where collectors are particular, as they tend to try and track down the rarer colours. Pink, blood red and cobalt blue are amongst the rarest but the one that collectors

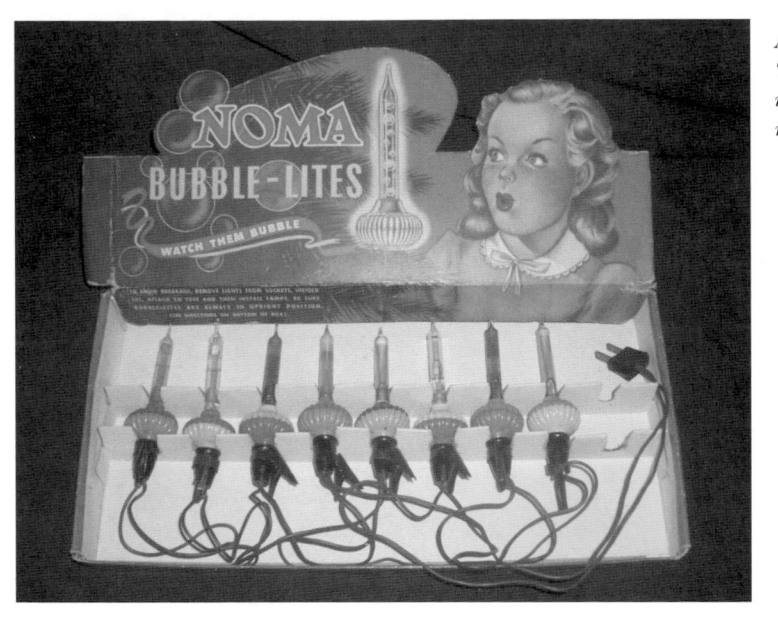

A box of vintage Noma 'Bubble Lights', unfortunately missing the rare coloured purple one.

desperately seek is purple. This particular colour was only available for the first three years of manufacturing. However, the slight problem with sourcing the colours is that because of the age of these lights the liquid over the years has darkened and it can be difficult to distinguish a true purple light. I have seen them for sale, with sets in good condition making £50-£100 if they have the purple light inside.

In 1948 NOMA changed the style of their lamps because so many people were copying them. The saucer shape was released but unfortunately was susceptible to heat damage, so was discontinued almost straight away and the company went back to the biscuit-style.

Individual lights are also something that a collector looks for and with NOMA it is the very rare rocket light designed by Frank Pettit, which was only made for two years in 1961 and 1962. This particular design was inspired by the space programmes in operation during this period.

KRISTAL SNOW

One of the companies that decided they too wanted to cash in on the bubble light phenomenon was Paramount. They named their bubble lights 'Kristal Snow Animated Candles' and changed the NOMA spelling of 'Bubble Lites' to 'Bubbling Lights'. Another difference was that they filled their lights with oil and pumice rather than the methylene chloride. This resulted in the bubbles being a lot finer and smaller which were difficult to see and get the desired effect when displayed on a Christmas tree. Due to this adaptation to manufacturing, Paramount lights were not as popular with the people as the NOMA ones and so today are extremely scarce.

RARE BUBBLES

Goodlite was another manufacturer who copied NOMA's designs by producing the Shooting Star bubbling lights. Again these lights are hard to come by as they were not of the same quality and so were not particularly good sellers at the time.

Peerless produced a candelabra set of lights; over the years much of the liquid in these lights has faded to become clear so if you manage to find a set that still has the coloured liquid they can command a premium with collectors.

Sparkling Royalties by Royal sold well when released in 1947 however collectors are keen to own the later 1948 Royal Crown candelabra lights. The more sought after boxes are those with the mixed colour bases as many of the lights produced had the same colour bases. They also produced Snowmen and Santa Claus figures holding a bubble light in these candelabra designed lights. Very few of these box sets have survived and so again are real collectors' pieces.

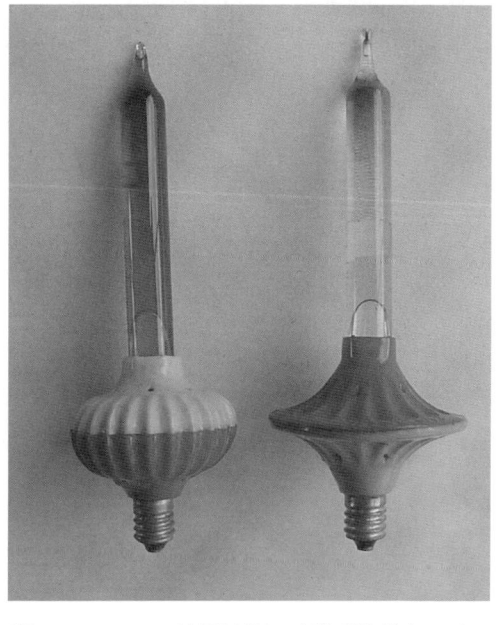

The more common NOMA 'Biscuit' bubble light and the 1948 NOMA 'Saucer' bubble light.

Alps was made by a Japanese company and unlike other manufacturers did not use the plastic base but instead an outside figural lamp base with the tube attached to the top. This particular design did not work properly as not only was it delicate and easily broken but the heat did not transfer properly. Due to the manufacturing complications, these lights did not appear for any length of time and so today are amongst the rarest for collectors.

Polly Snap On was made in the late 1940s: this bulb had a ribbed glass tube which was something totally different to the other bubble lights that had been produced. It also had outstretched holly leaves around the base. Unfortunately many were heat damaged making them hard to find today.

Seda Snap On was produced for just one year from 1950; much like the 'Polly Snap On' this light was also decorated with outstretched holly leaves. A rare light to track down, it is even harder to find them with all the leaves still intact as quite often they were broken off due to the brittleness of the plastic.

Telsen Bubble Lights The bubble light was a roaring success in America but not so much in Britain. This was mainly due to the fact that they were expensive to buy and the British people just didn't have the money to spend on such luxuries so soon after the War. However, the Telsen Electrical Company based in Manchester did manufacture

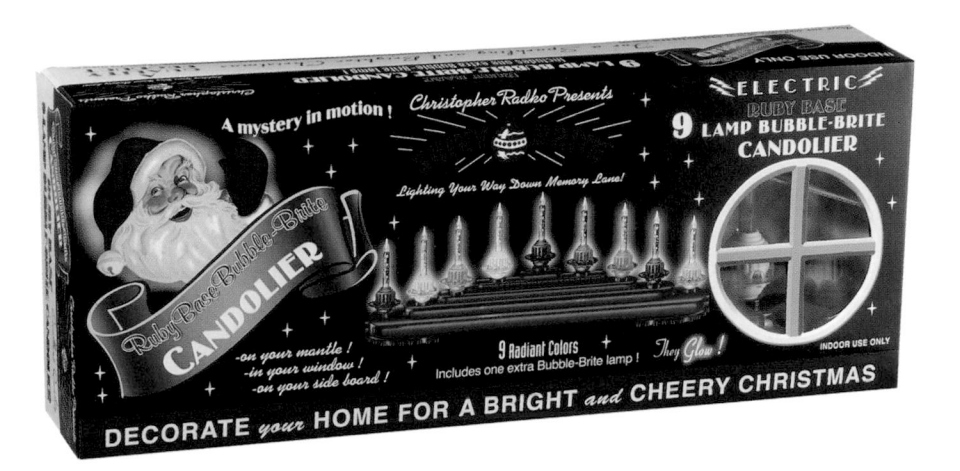

A Christopher Radko 'Shiny Brite' set of modern 'Bubble Brite' lights.

bubble lights and you can find some of these British examples today on the collectors' market.

In collecting terms there are so many variations on the vintage bubble light design and various different manufacturers that it makes collecting Christmas tree lights very complex. A subject that stands alone, as well as forming part of Christmas collectables, there are many who specialise in amassing just this particular design of Christmas light. You can still buy modern bubble Christmas tree lights today, although they are a little fancier with some having glitter added inside to make them sparkle more. The modern ones are also made from acrylic or other hard plastic rather than the original glass tubes. As with any collecting category rareness is what strives a collector forward, and it is the vintage examples that catch the collector's eye; all hoping that one day they will find that elusive piece or at the very least a purple NOMA 'Bubble Lite'.

CHARACTER COLLECTABLE LIGHTING

Aside from plain bulbs many companies started to manufacture lights under licence. Possibly the most well known being the NOMA 'Mickey Mouse' bell set which became available from 1936. These gorgeous bell lights were created in order to encourage children to buy lights not just for Christmas trees but for parties as well. Today this particular set is one of the most well known collectables in Christmas lighting and boxes usually sell for around £50-£60. Other sets produced by NOMA were the 'Disney Silly Symphonies' and a set of 'Fairy Tales'. All were the exact same bell lights made of heavy-duty plastic but with different images applied to them. Popeye was also a favoured character and a few companies such as Reliance produced bell light sets featuring this muscle-bound sailor's antics.

The famous 'Mickey Mouse' lights dating to the 1930s with the Mazda trademark name.

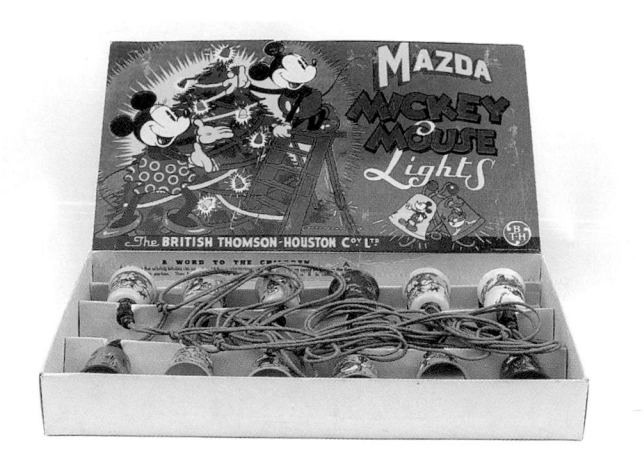

CHILDHOOD MEMORIES

From the 1950s onwards, it was customary for every home to have their trees and their house decorated with Christmas lights and by this time there were just so many to choose from. The introduction of the midget bulbs, otherwise known as the fairy lights became popular, as did strings of larger lights. I remember as a child hanging large lanterns onto the tree, there would only be around ten to twelve lights on the string so the tree looked a little bare unless you hung loads. Another set I remember is that of 'Cinderella' by Pifco. There were twenty lights on the string, which consisted of ten lanterns and ten Cinderella coaches. Quite big and really ornate they were framed in gold plastic and were bright pinks, yellows, greens and blues. I used to always take my time placing them around the tree because in my young eyes they truly were fairytale lights.

Today, these later lights are just as collectable as some of the earlier ones. There were many styles to choose from including Christmas inspired designs. 'Matchless Stars', which look very much like the more modern style lights you find today, came onto the market in 1935 and were in production until the 1950s. Collectors are keen to acquire these earlier designs as well as those lights that have a novelty value.

I often wonder what happened to the

The light manufacturer Pifco issued many different styles of Christmas tree lighting.

'Matchless Stars' were first introduced in 1935 and remained on the market until the 1950s and usually had real crystal points.

'Cinderella' lights from my childhood – I presume they were thrown away, and this is the reason that today these lights have become so highly sought after.

Box Clever

Even though many of these lights are highly collected items in their own right, we must not forget the wonderful packaging that these sets were sold in. Many showed images of fresh-faced children smiling up at a twinkling light on a Christmas tree, whilst others depicted Christmas figural characters. Epitomising their era, this early packaging is not just sought after by collectors of Christmas lights but also of Christmas collectors in general, as well as crossing over to those that adore the nostalgic images on packaging of days gone by.

Up to Date

Technology has advanced considerably and the most common lights today are the LED (light-emitting diode) ones. The majority of which have flasher or interrupter bulbs so are able to twinkle in different rhythmic patterns. We mustn't forget fibre optic lights which glisten bright colours, and if you want to get really advanced there are laser lights. All of which are a breakthrough in the lighting business.

Nowadays, festive lights are produced in large numbers and there are so many varieties to choose from. So which lights should you be storing away for future years that will become collectable? I recommend buying those that already have collectable appeal, which are sure to become even more desirable in the future. Look at the licensed lighting products such as the latest Disney film or hit television show. Novelty always stands the test of time and the more innovative the design the better investment for the future.

Very rare celluloid Christmas lights in the form of a dog, sheep and hard to find polar bear.

Christmas Light Facts

- Before the introduction of the Victorian illumination lamp candle holders, people would pierce tins with holes so the light from the candle would shine through.
- Christmas lights were extremely expensive when first issued so people had the opportunity to rent them from stores.
- Early figural light bulbs were of flowers, fruits and Christmas figures, these were mould-blown and usually painted by toy makers.
- Very early lights were made of various materials including celluloid.
- Japan and America were the leading market manufacturers of Christmas tree lights.
- The fairy lights today are still wired the same way as the vintage ones, if one goes out so does the whole lot – so fast moving technology hasn't solved this problem.

CHAPTER 3

DESIRABLE DECORATIONS

I always admire a tree when strung with lights but it still never looks quite as special as when covered in all those glorious colourful decorations. Once again this particular task is down to personal taste with some people preferring the more traditional glass baubles, beads, tinsel and sweets whilst others use the abundance of novelty decorations which can be bought readily in the shops today. Then there are people whom smother their trees with anything and everything, whilst the minimalists tastefully add just a few classy decorations. To be honest, it doesn't matter which way you decide to partake in this festive tradition as long as once it's done you can stand back and be proud of your efforts knowing that your tree looks exactly how you envisaged it.

IN THE BEGINNING

It wasn't always tinsel and baubles in fact that came much later – however the decoration of trees and bushes dates back to ancient man as they believed the spirits would be attracted to the decorations and keep them away from their homes during the winter months. Later people made a complete turnaround and would bring evergreens such as holly, mistletoe and ivy into their homes to give shelter to the spirits of nature.

Whereas today, through superstition we take down our decorations by Twelfth Night, people used to leave theirs up until Candlemas, which falls on 2nd February. This meant that the spirits would be kept from shelter in people's homes until spring had arrived when the spirits would again be able to return to the outside. Another superstition during medieval times was that people believed if they did not dispose of their evergreens by spring then the little spirits would cause chaos in their homes until they were set free.

FRUIT TO GINGERBREAD MEN

Fruit, nuts and candies were the earliest commercial decorations on a tree. This was first started in Germany and even today these foods are associated with the celebrations. In German markets gingerbread man makers would cook the biscuits with raw honey directly

People believed that if they took evergreens into their home during the winter they were protecting the spirits.

from the honeycomb. They soon realised that this left a lot of wax and instead of wasting it they learnt how to clean, and then press the wax into carved moulds. The shapes were mainly of cherubs and angels and just before the wax hardened they would secure a ribbon onto the decoration then paint it. Once the decorations were ready they were sold as 'fairings' – Christmas fair souvenirs. People would then buy them, take them home and tie them onto the Christmas tree.

VICTORIAN SCRAPS

From the early 1800s publishers produced uncoloured or, at slightly more cost, hand coloured picture sheets. Most were elaborately embossed or simply matt finished and they were intended to be coloured in by children and then cut out. Most bought these sheets with their pocket money and would spend hours of enjoyment colouring in the numerous figures and designs. Originally these scraps were used by German bakers to

Makers of gingerbread biscuits discovered they could create Christmas decorations from the raw honey wax that was left over after the biscuits had been made.

Children and adults would decorate their Christmas trees with colourful paper scraps.

decorate cakes. They were also used as decorative additions to Christmas and Valentine cards as well as being used on the Christmas tree as home-made decorations.

HOME-MADE DECORATIONS

The other things that people used to decorate their Christmas trees were home-made. These consisted of small toys, carved wooden shapes, pierced tin stars, paper decoration such as gold paper cornucopias and something that we still use to this day – tinsel.

TANTALISING TINSEL

FACT
The tinsel-making machine was invented in 1610 and only the wealthy could afford to decorate their trees with this real shimmering silver.

You either love it, or you hate it: but whatever your preference, tinsel has an interesting history and is one of the most common traditions for Christmas. Personally – I quite like a little around the house and tend to place some on my trees as it adds a colourful effect.

Originally tinsel was made out of real silver by machinery that would press the silver into thin strips. Although an incredibly durable material it did tarnish easily especially when placed near the real candles as the smoke would cause discolouration. Because of this problem in later years tinsel was created from tin alloy as well as pewter.

We believe that this festive decoration was invented around the 1600s but know very little about who invented it and why, however, it does have a German name *Lametta*, a diminutive form of the Italian word Lama, which translates to blade.

By the 1920s icicle tinsel was popular as a tree decoration – a much nicer alternative than today's made from plastic foil or aluminium.

TINSEL TREE DECORATIONS

Now the reason I mention tinsel isn't because it is easy to come by as a collectable but because many early German tree ornaments were actually made from it. Obviously early tinsel made of silver is near impossible to track down but the later ornaments have a huge following. The majority of these tinsel decorations consist of shapes made from wire which then have the tinsel wrapped around the frame; early ones are made of just the tinsel but later ornaments started to appear with decorative glass beads and baubles woven into the designs. This particular style of tree ornaments were used right up until the 1960s and today are amongst the easiest examples to track down costing just a couple of pounds each.

TRADITIONAL GLASS BAUBLES

One of the earliest forms of commercial decorations was glass beads made in Bohemia and along the borders of Germany

Many German tree ornaments were made from tinsel. Wrapped around wire and then shaped they made stunning tree decorations.

in Thuringia, Lauscha during the Seventeenth Century. The male glass blowers had a rather strong liking for ale so when intoxicated with the drink they would have competitions to see who could blow the largest ball. This meant that as the glass ball grew it would generally explode, so their wives would gather together the broken bits, take them home and decorate the insides with a silver nitrate solution. Then they would sell them at the markets as Christmas balls that would keep the spirits away. (Strange that it was under the influence of spirits which caused this form of early decoration in the first place!)

By 1863 gas had become available so glass blowers were able to blow much thinner glass that wouldn't explode easily. They soon realised that glass could also be blown into wooden moulds, and so began to create varies shapes and figural glass ornaments. Lauscha became the hub of Christmas ornamentation, with generations of families all working to produce different things for this Yuletide season.

It wasn't long before these new decorations were being exported to both Britain and America. The first person to import the decorations on mass to the States was FW Woolworth; one of the biggest department stores until 2009 Woolworths was, an institution in British shopping.

When first available to the public, these glass bauble decorations were extremely expensive to buy and so only the very rich could afford to decorate their Christmas trees with them.

A display of various tree decorations dating from Victorian to Twentieth Century.

Because of this reason the beautiful glass coloured balls became a symbol of status – the more glass ornamentation that decorated your tree the higher up the class scale you climbed.

However, by the 1890s this festive idea had taken off and nearly everyone could afford these glass decorations so many Christmas trees were laden with these decorative glass ornaments ensuring that their trees would glow, twinkle, glitter and sparkle!

Today there are many varied kinds of Christmas tree baubles, and decorations have become a huge hub for collecting.

What to Look For

There are two main periods that collectors tend to prefer when sourcing vintage Christmas ornaments those that date to the Victorian period and the middle of the Twentieth Century. There are also many different varieties of decorations from these particular eras including those made from glass, embossed paper, tin and plastic. Each also varies in price dependent on condition, age and materials. You can still pick up some examples for a few pounds but if looking for really good examples such as the Victorian embossed paper ones made by Dresden then you need to start thinking a lot higher in monetary terms.

A Victorian Christmas

Victorian Christmas tree branches were alight with all sorts of wonderful ornaments that reflected the opulent decorating style of the time. Most Christmas trees of this period would have a variety of different ornaments from various shaped thin blown glass figurines to large heavy glass balls and exquisite paper decorations to pressed tin displays.

German Kugels

The heavy glass balls or globes are known as 'Kugels' which when translated from German simply means ball or sphere. The original German balls are what collectors crave and these tend to be made of thicker glass with decorative metal tops. Early examples of the 'Kugels' were generally too heavy to hang from the branches of a Christmas tree so instead were suspended from ceilings. However, the Germans soon latched on to the fact that they could be made smaller in order that they could be displayed on the tree. Originally they were made in various shaped guises such as bunches of grapes, apples and pears. These original ones are what collectors seek and the grapes which date to around the 1890s sell for between £100 and £150 each, especially if vibrant colours such as green and blue.

French Kugels

By the 1920s the French had realised that they could also make the 'Kugels' and started blowing them in various beautiful swirling colours. These French decorations were much lighter than the German ones and the caps are very art deco in design. The main company

Translated the Kugel means 'ball' or 'sphere' in German.

to create these beautiful glass balls was Vergo Glass just outside of Nancy. You can distinguish these French alternatives by their weight and the fact that each one carries VG1721 on the cap. Vergo ceased production these balls in the 1930s so this particular maker is sought after. The important thing to bear in mind when collecting the French variety is that the collectability is in the different colour ways. The most common is silver whilst a rarer colourway to find is red or purple which are difficult to track down.

Collecting Tip
Make sure that when you buy an antique 'Kugel' it still has its cap secured, if loose do not try and pull out as this devalues the 'Kugel' itself quite considerably.

MODERN KUGELS

'Kugels' are still being made today especially in European countries but they are not just for displaying at Christmas. Depending on the glass factory and blower you can buy egg-shaped ones for Easter and hearts for Valentines. There is also a market for modern 'Kugels' in America although the balls are often referred to as Friendship or Witches balls.

A selection of genuine vintage 'Kugels' displaying their original caps.

Spot a Vintage Kugel

- Original 'Kugels' are made of very heavy glass, too heavy for Christmas tree branches.
- The colour of the 'Kugel' is decorated from inside the ornament (the lining) unlike modern ones which are blown coloured glass.
- Vintage 'Kugels' tend to have random spotting where with age the colour has rubbed.
- Sometimes the caps on the 'Kugel' have silver loss or are rubbed with age.
- Original 'Kugels' have a wonderful lustre and patina which comes with age.

BUYER BEWARE
Learn as much as you can before buying antique 'Kugels' as unscrupulous dealers have been known to switch the caps between old and new pieces. Make sure you buy from a reputable dealer who can guarantee that the piece is genuine vintage.

VICTORIAN PAPER DRESDEN DECORATIONS

The paper tree ornaments were also popular with the Victorians, especially the fabulous ones produced in Dresden, Germany. Whilst fellow Germans were blowing glass in Lausha, in the 1880s the people of Dresden decided they too would produce Christmas tree decorations. Using embossed and pressed paper as well as cardboard they created a whole host of different shapes to hang on the tree. There were fish, animals, moons, rocking horses, storks and even polar bears amongst the designs. Literally anything you can think of was made into a tree decoration.

There were three different kinds of Dresden paper ornaments available which included:

An embossed paper Dresden ornament in the form of Father Christmas.

Flat Dresden – The paper flat ornaments which were embossed on just one side with the reverse being painted.

Double Dresden – These were coloured and embossed on both sides. Some were mirror images of each side glued together whilst the others had a front and a back of the figure. So when assembled they completed the image.

Three-dimensional Dresden – The hardest to make they were made up of small pieces, then like a jigsaw puzzle were placed together. This was usually done by cottage workers who waited until the pieces were dry then took them home to assemble. The attractive thing about these Dresden pieces is that they could actually stand up by themselves.

The Double Dresden ornaments were sometimes mirror images of each side.

Beautiful three-dimensional Dresden paper ornaments in the form of a horse's hoof, birds and a horse carriage.

TRICKY TECHNIQUES

In order to actually make the Dresden paper decorations the cardboard was dampened so that it was flexible enough to work with. Then the design shape was stamped out. Some were then painted, although most were embossed with gold and silver. In order for each decoration to be made there was a need for two dies. The first called a stamping die carved the shape of the design whilst the second one, a receiving die carved a negative of the design. On the stamping die the detail was raised, whilst the receiving die had an identical matching depression. A complicated process: each ornament that was double-sided required four dies whilst a three-dimensional ornament needed two for each section.

Each of these decorations possessed an amazing amount of detail, were extremely ornate, and decorated in amazing vivid colours even to the point of being garish. Whereas Christmas decorations were already expensive which only the rich could afford, the Dresden works of art were extortionate but did look wonderful on the tree.

Even though these decorations were produced in their thousands very few actually still remain today making them very collectable. You can expect to pay around £80 for a flat paper antique Dresden but quite a bit more if you can find a three-dimensional one. As with the 'Kugels' these Dresden designs are being made for today's modern market with original

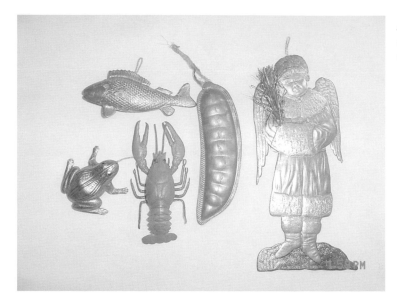

A wonderful cross section of Dresden ornaments in a variety of designs.

vintage materials, the perfect alternative if you can't find or afford the genuine article: but if you can lay your hands on an antique decoration in good condition, then it is a prized find ensuring that any collector of Christmas decorations will become green with envy.

VICTORIAN PRESSED TIN

The other decorations to adorn the tree during the Victorian era were those made of pressed tin. Brightly coloured, once again, they had lithograph surfaces and are very much like the German tin toys of the time.

1920S AND 1930S

By the 1920s and 1930s glass ornaments were the most popular decorations and were being imported mostly from Germany in tremendous volumes. They also came in many forms and included fruit and vegetable designs to figural, and Christmas characters to floral. Decorations shaped like vehicles were also popular as were zeppelins. They all came in an assortment of colours with flocked, glittered, silvered and shiny matt external decoration.

A SHINY BRITE CHRISTMAS

Much changed after the First World War as Germany no longer exported Christmas decorations to Europe and the United States. The Christmas market started to become a prolific industry across the world and slowly manufacturers from other countries began to produce wonderful examples of decorations. One such manufacturer was Corning New York. They already had a machine that made light bulbs out of ribbons of glass (this machine is on perma-

Various German and Italian glass decorations hanging on a pink feather tree. Dating from the 1920s to the 1950s.

nent display in the Henry Ford Museum in America) so Woolworths decided to ask if they would use this machine to make glass Christmas ornaments. Corning agreed and soon was able to mass-produce the ornaments: as many as 300,000 per day. One of their biggest customers was a man named, Max Eckhardt, a German immigrant who owned a company named Shiny Brite. Eckhardt would purchase the ornaments, lacquer them by machine, before hand decorating to sell on.

Wartime shortages made the materials needed for creating the Christmas glass balls hard to come by so Shiny Brite would decorate clear balls with thin strips of colours instead of using the metallic oxide pigment that they had used to lacquer in the past. As a result of this new decoration method Shiny Brite ornaments became very popular as the ornaments were unique. By the end of the war they were the largest manufacturers of Christmas ornaments in the world, which continued throughout the 1950s.

A Christopher Radko Shiny Christmas

In the 1960s Shiny Brite glass ornaments were not selling particularly well and by the 1970s they had stopped the production of glass ornaments altogether. Today it is these original vintage glass ornaments that collectors want to find as they bring back nostalgic memories of childhood. You can buy boxes for around upwards of £20 by sourcing them on internet auctions, at flea markets and boot sales: but don't dismay if you are unable to find the ones you are looking for as American Collectables Company Christopher Radko acquired the licence to carry on the tradition and produce gorgeous modern Shiny Brite decorations identical to the vintage examples.

These modern Shiny Brite ornaments were first introduced under the Christopher Radko brand in the autumn of 2001 and have had a huge collectors' following in their own right ever since. This is mainly due to collector's demand. Starting at around upwards of £15 a box, they certainly have the vintage look and come in wonderful vintage-style packaging.

Aside from the range of Shiny Brite ornaments under the Christopher Radko umbrella there is also a core line of traditional-style glass tree decorations that are manufactured in Poland, Germany, Romania, Czech Republic and Italy. Each of these ornaments is crafted by hand and takes up to seven days for each piece to be produced to the highest standard. These talented craftsmen start by carving the chosen design in clay or plaster, it is then given to a mould maker who using renaissance-era techniques creates a sand cast mould from molten metal. This then becomes the master mould and the making of glass ornaments can commence.

A boxed set of the modern Radko Shiny Brite flocked signature Christmas tree baubles.

A Week to make a Decoration (this applies to core glass only and not the Shiny Brite range)

I think the most appealing factor for collectors is that Christopher Radko range of core glass ornaments are all handmade with each one taking exactly seven days to perfect.

The glassmaker is responsible for the first stage after the master mould has been created. Using strong high-grade tempered glass a decoration shape is created by the glass-blower into the mould. You can always tell that it is a Christopher Radko ornament because the decoration is a lot heavier and is quite solid to touch as opposed to other decoration makers who tend to use lower grade glass which is not as strong and is easily broken.

On the second day the decoration is injected with liquid silver, this gives the decoration their luminescence and is what makes Christopher Radko ornaments totally unique.

The third day is when the matt lacquer is hand applied. This is the main body of colouring – so if it is a glass ornament in the form of Father Christmas the matt lacquer is applied in red.

A second coat of lacquer is then applied on day four, as are the other main colours required to decorate the main body of the ornament.

Day five is when the finer painted details are added by hand, this could be eyes, or even seeds on a fruit. This is an extremely skilled job and as with anything that is hand manufactured it adds collectability as no two pieces are alike.

No Christmas ornament would be complete without a dusting of glitter and this is what takes place on the sixth day.

The seventh day and during the final stages each ornament is quality inspected and then the Radko charm and custom designed ornament crown (finial) is added. This finial reads R-A-D-K-O so you can always distinguish between a true Radko ornament and a lesser quality copy. The ornaments are then tagged and packed for shipping.

These beautiful decorations come in hundreds of different shapes, sizes and designs meaning there are many to choose from. A combination of vintage style with modern contemporary design these tree decorations are not only highly collectable but also 'Works of Heart'.

The core line glass Christopher Radko ornaments take seven days each to make as they are all handcrafted.

My sweet little TY 'Holiday Bear' always adorns my Christmas tree.

MODERN COLLECTABLES

Aside from the Christopher Radko ornaments there are a whole host of modern tree decorations available for collectors. Every year manufacturers cash in on Christmas by producing special or limited edition pieces that can only be bought during the seasonal period. As a result demand is high because collectors clamour to own them.

The golden motto that I use throughout collecting is 'Only buy it if you love it!' there is no point purchasing something in the hope that it might become a future collectable if you can't bear living with it. The same applies to anything you might decide to buy for decorating the Christmas tree. If it gives

Modern tree ornaments come in all shapes and sizes with some based on popular cartoon and film characters like these resin Betty Boop tree decorations which I own.

you pleasure once it is hanging from the branches then it is a sound investment, otherwise just don't buy it. I must admit though I have a strange array of items on mine including a tree-hanging TY 'Holiday Bear' beanie which is decorated with holly – although once a collecting phenomenon, now you can't even sell TY beanies at a boot sale and many people have black sacks full of them in their attic, unsure what to do with them next. However, I think my small beanie bear wearing his Christmas hat looks really sweet hanging on the tree – so every year out he comes again.

I also own some resin-made Betty Boop tree decorations which were bought for me one year by a friend and an array of Disney, Warner Brothers and other character collectable plastic figures. A complete mismatch of delights, when thrown together they look amazing on the tree.

There is just so much on offer when it comes to modern tree decorations that it is difficult to know where to start, and indeed where to stop. Nearly every manufacturer will make something to celebrate the festive season so it really is a question of knowing what to buy. I cannot possibly cover them all so have decided to share with you my favourites – the ones that I feel have already become a collectable success or certainly will do in the future.

A Crystal Christmas

Swarvoski Crystal was founded by Austrian jewellery and glass-cutter, Daniel Swarovski. He patented an electric cutting machine in 1892 which facilitated the production of lead crystal glass. Today, the Swarovski ranges include crystal jewellery and sculptures. Their logo stamped on each piece was originally an edelweiss flower but this was replaced by a swan in 1988.

Highly collectable, each year Swarovski produce special annual edition Christmas tree hanging ornaments. In 2008 it was a Christmas Snowflake which hung on a blue satin ribbon.

The 'Christmas Set' was also released in the same year, which comprised of two smaller snowflake ornaments and the larger special annual one. A special 'Angel' ornament was also available. Made of fully faceted clear crystal, she had a matt finish to her hands and head and was fixed with a satin ribbon so she could be hung onto the tree branches. Retailing at £70 I can hear you all

Sparkling in a million ways this Swarovski Christmas tree snowflake ornament was the annual piece for 2008.

The Christmas tree set produced by Swarovski consisted of the large annual piece and two smaller snowflake hanging ornaments.

saying that this is a lot to pay for a Christmas tree ornament but if you aren't too worried about buying the special annual pieces then Swarovski also releases other Christmas inspired decorations, such as the 'Ice Flower' hanging ornament which could double up as a napkin holder and only costs £35.

FACT
Marilyn Monroe wore a skin-tight evening gown dripping with 6,000 Swarovski crystals while singing 'Happy Birthday' to John F Kennedy at Madison Square Gardens in 1962. The dress fetched $1.2 million at a Christie's Auction in 1999.

Tiffany Tree Temptations

Well-known jewellery and giftware manufacturer Tiffany also produces some wonderful tree hanging ornaments around the holiday period. Once again, made from crystal they have bright red ribbons tied onto them so they can be hung on the tree. Designs vary but in recent years there has been a snowman, a star and a porcelain Christmas holiday wreath which retailed at £30. Prices start from around £30 if buying directly from Tiffany or alternatively you can seek them out on internet auctions.

TOP TIP
Buy your collectable tree decorations out of season on internet auctions as prices tend to dip a little then shoot back up once the Christmas season starts.

Ceramic Collectables

Many ceramic and porcelain manufacturers release special piece designs around the festive period which include an array of wonderful hanging tree ornaments. Not only do these highly collectable designs look stunning hanging on the tree but some of them are also worth a pretty penny.

Royal Doulton Bunnykins

In 1934 a nun by the name of Barbara Vernon sketched scenes of delightful bunny rabbits participating in human activities. These sketches caught the eye of her father Cuthbert Bailey who at the time worked as general manager for the British pottery firm Royal Doulton. These sketches were adapted for production on a range of nursery-ware, which proved hugely successful so in 1939 the first modelled figurines were created. Extremely rare these large figures entitled Mary, Billy, Reggie, Freddie, Farmer and Mother Bunnykins are amongst the most sought after of all the Bunnykins figurines. However the smaller figurines we know and love today were not

The very scarce Royal Doulton Santa Bunnykins tree ornament designed by Harry Sales and modelled by David Lyttleton.

placed into production until 1972. An immediate success, over thirty years on they still have a faithful following from collectors all around the world.

In the past Royal Doulton have produced some flat ceramic plaque Bunnykins tree hanging ornaments with one of the most popular being the 1994 'Trimming the Tree'. This disc-style tree ornament depicts two female bunnies hanging all the ornaments on the branches on their Christmas tree. These are fairly inexpensive to buy at around £15 to £20 each.

In 2005 two sets of three-dimensional figural hanging ornaments were issued. Each set was comprised of four Bunnykins figures which could be hung by their attached ribbons. The first set was of Father Christmas, an elf, Christmas Busker and Christmas Eve. The second set consisted of Mother Christmas, Christmas Angel, Carol Singer and one entitled just 'Christmas'.

However, one of the rarest figural hanging tree ornaments you can find from the Royal Doulton Bunnykins range is DB62 which is named 'Santa Bunnykins Happy Christmas'. Issued in 1987 this three-dimensional figure was made specifically as a tree hanging ornament with a hole in his ear where the ribbon could be threaded. However, because of this purpose many didn't survive in one piece. Commissioned by American Express in a special limited edition size of 1,551 Santa Bunnykins was designed by Harry Sales and modelled by David Lyttleton. If you manage to find one this little bunny will set you back in the region of around £200 to £300. So if you are lucky enough to own one of these Santa Bunnykins figures and was planning on hanging him on the tree then make sure you place it very carefully as he could probably be the most expensive Christmas tree ornament you will ever own.

LLADRO

One of the most collectable porcelain factories is that of Lladro, which was founded in the 1950s by three brothers; Juan, Jose and Vincente Lladro. They began with a small workshop in Almacera, near the city of Valencia, Spain. However, this collectable manufacturer has grown so that their sculptures are now highly sought after by collectors from all over the world. Aside from the general ranges of wonderful figurines that they produce there are also many Christmas-inspired pieces which have, and still do include, tree-hanging ornaments. There are various types; from the annual matt porcelain tree baubles which can be bought for as little as £15 each on the secondary collectors' market, to the high glazed figurines of the Three Kings which were only produced during 1990 and sell for £50 to £80 per set. There is also an array of unusual Christmas tree hanging ornaments that have been produced by Lladro which include 'Little Roadster' (a porcelain model of a car) through to a rocking horse, decorative doll, and 'Little Harlequin'. All have ribbons attached for hanging and sell for between £15 and £30 each. So there really is an assortment of items available from this prestigious porcelain house, which would look stunning on anyone's Christmas tree.

Every year Lladro produce various tree ornaments including the more traditional looking annual baubles.

LILLIPUT LANE

Founded by David Tate in 1982, Lilliput Lane is well known amongst collectors for their intricate sculptures of vernacular English architecture. Created from resin rather than porcelain or ceramic, these miniature cottages are based on real British, American, German and Dutch cottages. There is much demand for new issues, especially in America, and those that have been retired.

Once again, Lilliput Lane also ensures there is a Christmas tree ornament available for collectors every year. Some are harder to find than others but in recent years there has been the 2007 releases entitled 'Mince Pie' (a cottage that literally resembles this festive morsel) and the 'Donkey Stable' in 2008, which was based on the Eighteenth Century thatched building at Chipping Walden (Saffron Walden) in the UK. There are also sets of decorative tree ornaments to collect each measuring 5cm in height. One such set consists of a baker's shop, a church, The Star Inn, and a miniature house, all covered with snow, of course. These sets tend to retail at around £20, which isn't a bad investment for four collectable tree ornaments.

GOEBEL AND HUMMEL DECORATIONS

Much like the Royal Doulton Bunnykins sketches another nun whose illustrations have become part of the collecting world are those by Sister Maria Innocentia (Berta) Hummel.

Lilliput Lane have produced many lovely Christmas tree hanging ornaments all in the form of their intricate sculptures of vernacular architecture.

Franz Goebel, the owner of the German porcelain company W Goebel Porzellanfabrik noticed Maria's work in a religious art shop. The result was that in 1935 the first set of Hummel figurines was released at the Leipzig Fair. A huge success the Hummel figurines were still being made for collectors after Maria passed away in 1946 aged just thirty-seven. Each piece made after her death had to be created true to Maria's original drawings and there remained a close link between the manufacturer Goebel and the Convent of Siessen where Maria had resided.

Of course the figurines are hugely popular and as with anything collectable are produced then discontinued. Like many companies they also created special annual Christmas pieces and their tree decorations have generally been in the form of Christmas or angel bells. The angel variety are usually available in many different colours. Some are plain white whilst others are vibrant yellow, red or blue, whereas the Christmas bell is generally white with a coloured raised decoration on the front.

GROLIER DISNEY ORNAMENTS

One of the largest manufacturers in Disney themed Christmas ornaments is the American company Grolier. Although more renowned as a publishing company they started in 1895 in Boston, USA. The company grew rapidly and was established in the UK in 1974. Aside from the children's books that are available through Grolier there is also a range of Disney Christmas tree decorations which have been specifically created for collectors. Each one is hand painted and specially designed by Disney. They can only be bought directly from Grolier, making them even more collectable as they cannot be bought in the shops. The variety of figures available is vast, ranging from Mickey Mouse to Winnie the Pooh and Donald Duck to Pluto. Each is made of hard plastic but once a year Grolier issue one special dated bisque ceramic ornament, which comes with a certificate of authenticity. These are the harder to find rare Grolier tree ornaments that collectors seek, however even the plastic examples are heavily collected both in the UK and America.

A KINKADE CHRISTMAS

Renowned as the 'Painter of Light', Thomas Kinkade is America's most successful living artist and is regarded as one of the foremost living painters of light. Born in 1958 Thomas was already an accomplished artist by the age of sixteen. After leaving college he started work in the film industry but in 1983 left this industry to pursue his ambition of becoming a painter of light-filled landscapes. Since achieving his vision Kinkade has received broad exposure and is increasingly popular. His paintings now receive six-figure sums and are collected by the rich and famous. His unique ability to capture the essence of light, which he recreates onto wonderful canvases, has opened up the path for an amazing selection of collectables.

Literally everything that Thomas Kinkade paints is transformed into some sort of collecting area. A devout Christian he adores the Christmas period and so of course there are a whole host of Kinkade Christmas collectables available.

When it comes to Christmas tree ornaments there are many to choose from and each is an individual work of art. In my own opinion, one of the most stunning are the 'Kinkade Sleigh Bells' baubles. Each is a light-reflecting silver colour sleigh bell which is hand painted with a Kinkade Victorian Christmas house scene on one side, the top of the bauble then drips with pure white snow and is topped with a sculptural Kinkade scene which has been hand-crafted from resin.

The range of elephant figurines, Tuskers are very collectable and each year lovely Christmas tree hanging ornaments are released.

However, each of the Kinkade decorations available to collectors has their own unique appeal. 'Jolly Ol' Soul' tree ornaments are three-dimensional ceramic ornaments which have been finished with twenty-two carat gold and glazed to give the look of glass. Included in the set of three are a traditional sleigh, festive Christmas tree and a jolly Santa. The unusual ingredient to these stunning decorations is that each is hand painted with a Kinkade scene, the sleigh has the painting on the side, Father Christmas has it on the edge of his coat, and the images are at the base of the Christmas tree. This wonderful effect enhances each of the ornaments, thus adding to the collectability.

COLLECTABLE CHRISTMAS

I have just touched on some of my own favourite modern collectables that are available for decorating the tree. However there are so many more worth sourcing that it is impossible to cover them all. Aside from the manufacturers themselves shops such as Past Times and mail-order companies like Bradford Exchange and Danbury Mint also have a huge selection of Christmas tree ornaments which they have commissioned especially from various manufacturers.

I have outlined below a selection of other collectable giftware companies who produce special seasonal tree decorations. Most of these can be found in local shops around the festive period or alternatively on the internet.

- Belleek
- Bronte
- Cherished Teddies
- Coalport
- Coca-Cola
- Gisela Graham
- Guinness Memorabilia
- Harrods
- Royal Copenhagen

- Royal Crown Derby
- Tuskers™
- Wedgwood

Harrods Department store in London has many special Christmas pieces available each year, the tree ornaments consist of miniature Harrods plush bears, various baubles and glass bear ornaments: most of which are exclusive to Harrods and cannot be bought anywhere else, thus having a huge collectors' following.

ORNAMENT ADORNED

No matter which way you decide to decorate your tree I am sure that once it is finished it will look fantastic. Although I usually opt for modern collectable items on one tree and vintage on another, there is nothing to stop you combining the two. The other nice thing about decorating your tree is that no one's will be identical as each of us puts our own mark, talents and vision into the perfect tree display, ensuring that each tree hung with decorations in people's homes is a unique collectable in its own right.

CHAPTER 4

THE FESTIVE FAIRY

Every little girl would like to be the fairy on the Christmas tree.

Gracie Fields

Although I love decorating my Christmas trees I am always left with a slight dilemma and that is what to place at the very top of the tree. Should I choose a shining star, wondrous angel or a festive fairy? A difficult choice it always has me stumped. As with everything about Christmas it is normally down to personal choice, there are those that feel that the star is the rightful symbol, whilst others like the idea of an angel but actually the fairy doll is much more of a British tradition and as we are talking about Christmas collectables it is the fairy that has the most collectable appeal.

WHY A FAIRY?

There are many theories as to why the British have a tradition of placing a fairy on the top of a Christmas tree although nobody seems to know for certain where it all began. Some believe that back in Seventeenth Century Germany it was traditional to top the tree with a model of the baby Jesus. Then in later years this was replaced by the figure of a male angel. It is said that the British who were not keen on adopting the German traditions swapped the angel to a fairy. This legend seems a little strange as pagans deemed these mystical wee folk as bad, and with the coming of Christianity fairies were reputed by the Church as being evil spirit creatures and not at all like the good mythological people of peace that we consider today.

Others believe that the tree-topping angels evolved into fairies because after the festive celebrations children would take down the angels and dress them in their doll's clothes. Thus, the original male angels would quickly be transformed by children's hands into female fairies.

Regardless of these theories, it doesn't really matter how the traditional use of the fairy on top of the Christmas tree began. The importance lies within the fact that it become customary for the British to place a fairy at the top of the tree (especially from the 1930s onwards) and so it has become a significant part of our historic British Christmas tradition.

The Fairy on the Christmas tree 1936 Gracie Fields song sheet.

CHILD'S PLAY

The Christmas fairy doll was seen as very special, and in many homes was gifted to a daughter or visiting young relative. The child whom received the beautiful fairy doll was extremely lucky and proud of her gift.

Early examples of fairy dolls were made from wax, papier mâché or porcelain. Many of the small bisque dolls were sold naked so that they could be dressed at home, although some manufacturers such as Armand Marseille did produce dressed dolls, which would cost in the region of £200 if you managed to find one today. During the early part of the Twentieth Century small dolls made from coarse white bisque were manufactured in Japan and imported to Britain; these also were sold as fairy tree-topper dolls.

German manufacturer, Armand Marseille produced dressed fairy dolls which today can cost in the region of £200.

CELLULOID

Another popular material used for making the fairy dolls in the early part of the Twentieth Century was celluloid (a highly flammable material made from nitrocellulose-based plastics and waxy white camphor.) Although extremely dangerous when placed near the naked flame of a candle many of these dolls have survived with the most common one still in existence having jointed arms, moulded all-in-one legs and body, large side-glance eyes and gold painted hair.

A popular material used for making dolls at the beginning of the Twentieth Century was celluloid.

COMPOSITION

A much safer option to the celluloid was the composition dolls (a mixture of plaster, sawdust and glue) which became fashionable during the 1920s and right up until the 1940s. Many manufacturers across the world began to make the dolls, with America producing the most. In Britain there were many manufacturers of the fairy doll including Rosebud, Roddy, Pedigree and Cascelloid (Palitoy). They created play dolls in all sizes, though in the main the composition fairies were around eight-inches in height because if they had been any bigger the tree would topple over. Although somewhat plain, these composition fairy dolls are worth seeking out and would look wonderful on top of your Christmas tree.

HARD PLASTIC MEMORIES

By the late 1940s hard plastic finally caused the demise of composition. If you placed the plastic near to a fire it wouldn't ignite (unlike celluloid) and if it became wet it wouldn't ruin the finish (unlike composition). The epitome of the English fairy doll these new hard plastic examples were not only child friendly but also inexpensive to buy. In England they were purchased from stores such as Woolworths and were how you would expect a Christmas fairy doll to look.

A German 1920s bisque doll made by Walther & Sohn with impressed W & S mark. She has composition limbs and is wearing an original golden thread headband, dress and undergarments.

A glittery wand in hand, these dolls were dressed in net, gauze, crêpe paper or muslin and were trimmed with tinsel and of course had magnificent glittery silver carded wings.

A prolific industry, many manufacturers such as Palitoy, Airfix, Pedigree and Rosebud created the dolls and even today they are still relatively inexpensive when found, so I think this is a great way for novice Christmas or doll collectors to learn about the various 1950s hard plastic fairy dolls without parting with too much money. Another major factor for collecting this particular area of Christmas is that it brings back for many people nostalgic childhood memories. My good friend and extremely knowledgeable doll expert Susan Brewer reminisces about her childhood fairy doll:

'I remember my mother buying a small fairy doll in the early 1950s, dressed in cerise-pink shiny card, with a matching pointed hat in the style of a medieval lady, with swirly wings. I was entranced as I had never seen a bright pink fairy before."

1960s Vinyl Dolls

Finally in the 1960s the first unbreakable doll was introduced. Made of vinyl, unlike hard plastic, it wouldn't shatter or crack. Children liked the feel of the new vinyl dolls and it was also inexpensive to manufacture. This new material also meant that hair could now be rooted as opposed to wigs being glued on to the heads. Many manufacturers started to make their fairy dolls from vinyl and these examples are readily collected by doll enthusiasts and Christmas collectors today.

Palmolive Soap Fairy Doll

Like today back in the 1950s many companies ran promotions where you could collect tokens to send off with a small amount of money and receive a piece of their advertising merchandise in return. In 1957 Palmolive soap ran a fairy doll promotion. Made by the

The 1957 Palmolive fairy doll was a huge success when run as a promotion in conjunction with Palmolive soap. She even came with a letter of apology about the fact that they had been inundated with orders.

British doll manufacturer Roddy, she was dressed in a white satin dress edged with silver braid, carried her faithful wand, and had long flowing blonde hair. Today this doll is a reasonably priced collectable; on her own you would only need to pay £10 to £12. However, if found with the original box and the letter which was sent accompanying the doll from Palmolive then you may need to part with double that amount.

ROSEBUD FAIRY

A major manufacturer of dolls in general was the British company Rosebud and their fairy dolls were extremely popular during the 1950s and 1960s. Some of their dolls did carry rather unusual expressions and did not appear particularly happy looking but instead had a bitter-looking face however many were also very pretty, pleasing dolls.

MISS ROSEBUD

The Miss Rosebud dressed jointed doll made of hard plastic was the perfect Christmas fairy to own in the 1950s. Also manufactured by Rosebud she carried the markings of Miss Rosebud on her back and was a really pretty-looking fairy doll. Measuring eight inches in height, she was dressed in a net sequin-scattered skirt with silver ribbon bodice and of course the wings were made of gauze. This particular model of doll is now quite hard to find and if you do manage to find one, especially if the doll is still wearing her original fairy outfit, be prepared to part with £100. However, of all the fairy dolls Miss Rosebud is one of my personal favourites, as her rounded red flushed cheeks and curly blonde hair is just how I imagine a child fairy to look and thus would appeal to real children – I can only guess that if you were the lucky child to receive this doll from the top of the Christmas tree then it would be your pride and joy.

AIRFIX FAIRY

When mentioning the company Airfix most people instantly associate them with plastic kit form aeroplanes and cars but they did make dolls as well. Once again a very cheap fairy doll to buy from toy shops and stores such as Woolworths, they only measured four inches in height and were dressed in crêpe paper or net skirts. Of course no fairy is complete without a wand and these small dolls also carried theirs. In fact it is the slightly later models of the Airfix fairy dolls that I remember from childhood. Although I wasn't actually born around this time, my grandma kept the same decorations for years and she used to top her tree with a small Airfix doll. I remember the large foil wings, huge gauze skirts and the most memorable decoration being the silver tinsel crown that she wore on her head. I used to love visiting my grandma, just staring for ages at the beautiful fairy on the top of the tree.

Airfix fairies measured around four inches in height and often wore crêpe paper or net skirts.

Thumbs up for the fairy

Another popular doll dating to the 1950s is the Roddy Thumbs Up fairy. Named because her thumbs were obviously pointing upwards she had chubby cheeks and a smiling mouth. The only slight problem was that her unusual thumbs up design made it a little difficult for her to hold her wand. Once again highly collected she is one to look out for, as she is slightly quirkier looking than some of the other fairy dolls.

Mother's Surprises

Many Christmas fairy dolls dating to the 1950s were dressed at home by mothers to present as Christmas surprises to their children. Even though they were not dressed in factory made clothes these dolls are still original and really delightful. Amongst the most popular fairy dolls to buy for home dressing were those by Tudor Rose. Cheap to buy, the majority were naked which allowed

The Tudor Rose dolls were often bought naked so that they could be dressed at home. Delightful dolls they have lovely faces.

people to then make their own outfits and this particular model of doll was perfect as a Christmas fairy as their faces were extremely fairy-like. In fact I find these Tudor Rose dolls most interesting when it comes to collecting as no two are ever the same. Also in my eyes, this is the essence of Christmas: children, and surprising them during this magical festive season. The home dressed dolls epitomise exactly what Christmas is all about and a Tudor Rose one is priced around £15 to £20 on the collectors' market. So please don't dismiss these dolls if you find one lurking in a collectables centre, or buried in a box at a boot sale because these dolls sum up the true meaning of children at Christmas time.

Moving On

The 1950s was probably the most exciting time for fairy dolls as there were so many different styles, designs and manufacturers to choose from. The fairy still remained popular throughout the 1960s and 1970s but most were imported from Hong Kong. Although lovely dolls they were not as elaborate as those manufactured in previous years and I believe that it was the hidden magic of the 1950s dolls that made them so desirable then and continues to grip the hearts of collectors today. This is why it's the examples dating to the 1950s that are eagerly sought after whilst the later ones although still collectable are not in as much demand.

The Fairy Demise

The fairy slowly started to disappear from the top of the Christmas tree around the 1980s. The angel was back with a vengeance and became available in all the shops. With moving technology these new vibrant angels were either fitted with musical mechanisms or had wonderful colour-changing lights. So quite suddenly the fairy fell out of favour and was replaced with the new en vogue angel.

Flower Fairies

FACT
Flower Fairies of the Spring was Cicely Mary Barker's first book, published in 1923 and brought her international acclaim.

Just because the Christmas tree-topper fairy doll wasn't as popular around the festive period didn't mean that modern manufacturers stopped making the fairy doll altogether. In 1983, the toy manufacturer Hornby, (better known for making trains) produced a whole range of small dainty Flower Fairies based on the illustrative Flower Fairy poems and books by the artist Cicely Mary Barker.

Originally just six dolls wearing colourful petal costumes were released in 1983. They

Hornby released a range of Flower Fairies based on Cicely Mary Barker's Fairy poems.

measured around six and a half inches in height and had delicate limbs a sweet face and Spock-like ears hidden beneath their beautiful rooted hair. Made from vinyl they had twisty waists, bendy knees and rotational hip joints. The early dolls were either blonde or brunette and they each had wings that fitted into their backs. Also available in this initial range were six costumes so that the fairy could change into another flower outfit if she wished. It made sense that one of the outfits was called Christmas. However, it wasn't long before the Christmas Fairy (the name changed later to Christmas Tree Fairy) also appeared as a dressed doll.

This particular Flower Fairy Christmas doll is relatively common to find now at boot sales and doll fairs. She originally wore a white pleated skirt with white top, lace sleeves and had a green ribbon tied crossover on the bodice. Her wings were peach in colour and she had brunette hair. This sweet fairy doll did undergo many variations though as the colour of her ribbon, dress length and skirt material often changed. Although not a true Christmas fairy tree topper, she still is a lovely Christmas inspired doll and fits nicely into the arena of collecting Christmas fairy dolls.

Another range that joined the Hornby Flower Fairies was that of Pixies. Again these cute little fellows had pointed ears and they possessed moulded, painted hair rather than rooted nylon locks. They accompanied the fairies and a Holly Pixie came packaged with the existing Christmas Fairy, although later he was available separately. He was extremely colourful and festive, with scarlet tights, a green tunic, which was decorated with holly leaves, a green hat and a belt of red holly berries. Today he is quite hard to find and so is sought after by collectors.

The Holly Pixie dressed in colourful festive scarlet tights and a green tunic is a very difficult doll to find.

Today there are many collectors of the Hornby Fairy dolls, all eager to source the most rare examples. Although they never really did replace the traditional Christmas fairy doll they are still deemed part of fairy doll collectables and so people continue to hunt them down to add to their collections.

FACT
In 1985 an animation film called *Star Fairies* based on the dolls was released and starred Drew Barrymore as the voice of Hillary.

ALBERON FAIRY

In recent years the manufacturer Alberon Dolls produced a porcelain version of the Christmas tree fairy as a limited edition. Quite a large doll she stands fourteen inches in height and wears a beautiful shiny iridescent short frock with matching wings whilst carrying a star-topped wand. This particular modern doll is quite heavy and placed on the top of the tree would probably topple it over. Collectors tend to use this particular Christmas fairy as a centrepiece for a Christmas table or just as decoration within the home.

CABBAGE PATCH FAIRY DOLLS

Another range of dolls that were produced for Christmas but were far too big and heavy to actually tie to the top of a tree were Cabbage Patch fairy dolls. Issued by Mattel during the 1990s within the range was the Holly Berry Fairy. She was dressed in an emerald green satin romper suit, also having an overskirt which was decorated with holly leaves. She possessed white wings, which were spotted with red holly berries, and a small holly motif on her cheek. Other Christmas fairy Cabbage Patch dolls: the Poinsettia Fairy in red, plus the Christmas Wish dressed in green with red striped sleeves, and the Snow Magic in white and blue.

Although in America there is no known tradition of using a Christmas fairy as a tree-

A more modern fairy doll is the beautifully porcelain Christmas Tree Fairy by Alberon Dolls although she would be far too heavy to place on top of the tree but makes a lovely decoration within the home.

topper Mattel did produce a special Cabbage Patch fairy doll for the United States market in Christmas 2000. The Holiday Scented Wal-Mart exclusive wore a white pleated iridescent dress trimmed with white fur and holly leaves. She also wore white leggings trimmed with fur and had chiffon wings sprinkled with gold sequins. The box bore a rhyme reading 'Holidays come once a year – here's a friend that's sweet and dear'. This small saying really does sum up the spirit of Christmas, as this time of year is all about the coming together of close friends and family.

WONDERFUL WANDS

Fairy wands are of course an important factor when it comes to fairy dolls; I mean how could they grant your wishes without one? Interestingly it seems that most of the fairy dolls from the 1950s and 1960s had identical wands, so there must have been one company who actually specialised in making fairy doll wands, which they would then sell to all the various doll companies. Made of a metal rod, with a cardboard star fixed to the top the wands measured around three to four inches in length. The star was also covered in glitter, which over the years sadly grew dull and faded. The later Airfix fairy, however, held a wand which had a plastic moulded star rather than the cardboard glitter one. So today if you are hunting out one of these fairy dolls try and make sure that she has her wand or if not track one down – your little fairy would be lost without it and of course this adds collectability – but at least you needn't worry too much about finding a special wand as most of the dolls from this period carried the same design.

MODERN FAIRY DOLLS

Today it is almost impossible to find a traditional Christmas fairy doll in the shops as people tend to top their trees with angels or stars. However there is one company that still produces a Christmas fairy doll and she is definitely worth getting if you are unable to hunt out the vintage dolls as she gives the desired look of a genuine old doll and still has collectable status.

Amanda Jane Dolls (www.amandajane dolls.com) offer a beautiful traditional-looking Christmas fairy doll made from vinyl who casts spells all over the place in her pink gossamer fairy outfit. This doll 'despite her

A more traditional modern offering is the Amanda Jane Christmas fairy doll. Made from vinyl she is wearing a lovely gossamer fairy outfit.

wings finds flying a wee bit hard' but lets face it nobody wants a fairy doll sitting on their tree that has a tendency to fly off at any given moment!

FOREVER THE FAIRY

After writing this chapter it has certainly made me realise that no Christmas is complete without a fairy doll. So there is no longer a dilemma as this tradition must be continued and not allowed to fade away – it will have to be a fairy perched on top of my trees each and every year from now on.

Chapter 5

ORNAMENTAL DECORATIONS

When it comes to Christmas decorations there are many of us that don't just stop at decorating the tree. Like plenty of you, I personally ensure there are collectable ornaments all around the house so that my home at Christmas really does have that festive grotto appeal.

I wind lights around the staircase, hang a wreath on the front door and have an abundance of ornaments in nearly every room – even the kitchen is adorned by some sort of Christmas crockery. I also love to scatter scented candles about the place so that when people visit they can smell Christmas cheer the minute they walk through the door.

Today, there are absolutely hundreds of collectable ornaments available to create the perfect Christmas atmosphere as each year manufacturers bring out new exciting seasonal-inspired pieces. These then quickly become highly sought after collector's items as they either sell out straight away or are discontinued once the Christmas celebrations have finished.

CHRISTMAS COLLECTING MANIA

As mentioned in my introduction (page 8) the best example of decorating a home at Christmas I have ever encountered was when I interviewed a gentleman in Bradford, England who turns his small cottage into a grotto every year. No nook or cranny remains undecorated in this cottage during the Yuletide festivities. Even the pictures on the wall are removed, wrapped in Christmas paper and then hung back up again so they resemble Christmas presents. Owning over one thousand Christmas items; from ceramics figures to resin models and Christmas train sets to candle snuffers, this particular collector is probably the most passionate that I have ever met when it comes to Christmas collecting and is prepared to travel the world in order to track down those elusive pieces to add to his ever-growing collection.

CHILDHOOD CHAINS

Things would have been quite different for this Christmas collector had he being trying to achieve the same effect decades before. There wasn't quite as much on offer from manufacturers as there is today and people would either make their own decorations or buy paper ones from shops like Woolworths.

Paper decorations were popular when I was a child, available in various shapes they were made from different coloured paper.

I remember as a child in the 1970s sitting for hours licking and sticking together coloured pieces of paper which would eventually turn into a long colourful paper chain. We used to have competitions to see who could make the longest and then once finished these paper chains would be secured to the ceiling from each corner to meet up in the middle.

Another thing that we would do is make our own house decorations from anything we could find; stars cut out of coloured foils, decorated shapes we had drawn with glitter, tiny empty boxes wrapped up with vibrant wrapping paper which would then be piled onto a table with a candle sitting in the middle as a cheap and effective table centrepiece.

I also remember shop-bought paper decorations during this period: one in particular was a large bell which was revealed in three-dimensional form once unfolded. Aside from bells these paper decorations came in various forms such as Christmas trees, angels and even just round paper balls. Some were just one colour whilst others were made up of different coloured papers. They looked fantastic when secured to the ceiling and most homes displayed these at Christmas time.

Following on from paper decorations were the coloured foil decorations, much the same as when unfolded they could be hung from the ceiling. You could also buy foil chains and door streamers, which again were available in numerous colours and styles.

MOVING INTO MODERN

Looking back to those paper and foil decorations seems a far cry from what we use now. Although you can still buy the foil variety in shops and sometimes find decorations made of paper (you can even still build your own paper chain, much like I did when I was a child) people don't tend to hang ornaments from their ceiling as much now as they used to.

House decorations are more common in the form of ornamental decorations which are strategically placed around the home and as nearly every collectable manufacturer has at some point released a Christmas-themed collectable there is much to choose from.

FIGURAL CHRISTMAS ORNAMENTS

From Lladro to Wade and Robert Harrop to Royal Doulton almost every collectable gift-ware company has at some point issued a special Christmas inspired ornament, making it almost impossible for me to cover every one. However, I have compiled together some of my own personal favourites which either epitomise the classical Christmas figure or have a more modern quirky slant on the seasonal scene.

ROBERT HARROP

The world of Robert Harrop designs are renowned for its 'Originality by design'. One of the most nostalgic collectables you will find on the market they specialise in producing resin figurines of our childhood favourite characters. You can choose between many figural ornaments, which include those of Andy Capp, *Camberwick Green* and *Mr Benn* as well as *Bagpuss*, *Magic Roundabout* and Dennis the Menace. Many of these characters have also been captured in festive guises such as the limited edition Windy Miller Festive Spirit a special limited edition Christmas tableau from the *Camberwick Green* range in 2008. Other collectable Christmas-themed Robert Harrop pieces include a tableau of Dennis the Menace and Gnasher shaking a Christmas tree. Entitled Christmas Capers this piece was released in 2007 and formed part of the *Beano* and *Dandy* range. Another successful line of figures produced by Robert Harrop is the Doggie People, again a limited edition piece released with the Christmas Time figurine featuring an Old English sheepdog dressed as Santa. Classed as one of the most popular collectable manufacturers of our time Robert Harrop pieces can also see huge returns on the collectors' market. The first ever *Camberwick Green* Christmas piece was released in 2002; entitled Christmas Post and limited to 1,000 pieces it originally retailed at £24.99. Within a few days this same design was exchanging hands on internet auctions for £400 to £500. If you manage to find this piece today, you will still need to part with around the same financial figure. However, the rarest of all the Robert Harrop Christmas figures was the Old English sheepdog, Santa, issued in 1996 through the Doggie People range. After producing just forty-one pieces with black boots, gloves and belt Robert Harrop realised that the copyright had not been placed onto the figurine. They then re-issued the model in a different colourway of brown boots, gloves and belt with the correct copyright details, thus making the forty-one initial pieces extremely rare.

TOP TIP
Join collectors' clubs in order to acquire special pieces, find out ahead of time what is due to be released and all the news and

Christmas Capers released in 2007 shows the amusing scene of Dennis the Menace and Gnasher shaking a Christmas tree.

information on the manufacturer. Robert Harrop's club was started in 1984 and each year they give their members a free figurine with their membership.

LLADRO

I mentioned in Christmas tree decorations (page 34) that the Spanish porcelain manufacturer Lladro each year release wonderful tree ornaments but this is just the tip of the iceberg for Christmas themed collectables from this company. They produce many figurines and tableau scenes with Christmas in mind and these are all eagerly collected. One of the most well-known ranges being The Night before Christmas and within this series there has been

Lladro 'Trimming the Tree' issued in 1992 and sculptured by Joan Coderch.

many Christmas figures released which include I Love Christmas (6672), a piece that was only available for one year (2000-2001) and featured a little boy standing on a stool admiring a Christmas ball decoration. This Christmas ornament tends to sell for around £150. Another lovely Christmas inspired tableau scene is entitled Trimming the Tree and features a girl hanging baubles on the tree whilst the boy has obviously just placed the star at the top and is asking the girl to admire it. This particular sculpture was released in 1992 and today costs around £500 to acquire.

Once again as with collecting anything only buy what you like. There is an abundance of different Christmas inspired pieces to choose from the Lladro pottery, both those that have been retired and are out of production as well as a constant stream of new releases each year. Perhaps you prefer to buy the more classical Christmas pieces or are drawn to the figurines that depict children. The choice is entirely up to you but whatever you choose you can be assured that when you buy a piece of Lladro you are not only purchasing a highly collectable figurine but also a wonderful piece of porcelain craftsmanship which is sure to increase in value over the years.

TOP TIP
When collecting Lladro make sure that it is of first quality (not a factory second). It is easy to distinguish between the two. A factory second has the Lladro tulip flower logo either ground out on the bottom or simply missing altogether so only buy pieces where you can clearly see the logo on the base.

WADE

Each year since 1997 the British collectables company Wade together with retailer C&S Collectables hold a Christmas extravaganza. This event is geared specifically towards collectors and is basically an open day where they can come along and meet other like-minded Wade enthusiasts and buy special Christmas inspired pieces.

This is a great way to amass highly collectable decorative Christmas ornaments, because if you don't attend the event it becomes very difficult to acquire a specific piece anywhere else at the original retail cost. This means that these special pieces tend to go up in value quicker than the figurines that can be obtained from general retail outlets and on internet auctions. Of course, there are a percentage of people that attend this event solely with the purpose of making a few extra pounds by listing them on internet auctions straight away but for the genuine Wade collectors to attend this event is a must.

Over the years there have been many pieces available at the Christmas bonanza in varied designs. 'Quakers on a Sleigh' was available in 2002 and in 2008 the Wade Collectors' Club offered collectors the chance to buy a limited edition Christmas Tetley tea folk piece called 'Gaffer decorating the tree'.

Another famed character to be recreated in ceramic from Wade is of the children's favourite animated character Snoopy. The 'Happy Holidays' limited edition Christmas figure was produced by C&S Collectables in 2000 and was modelled by C Roberts to celebrate the fiftieth anniversary of *Peanuts* (the name of the cartoon from which Snoopy was

'Happy Holidays' featuring the loveable character Snoopy was produced by Wade for C&S Collectables in the year 2000 as one of their Christmas pieces.

the star). If you manage to acquire this particular collectable figurine then expect to pay £30 to £50.

Although Wade is highly collected in its own right there are many Wade collectors who concentrate on just amassing the Christmas inspired ornaments. These collectors will travel from all over the world in order to attend the annual Christmas Bonanza so that they can add to their ever-growing collections. So it is worth being there yourself so that you too can get your hands on one of these delightful Christmas Wade ornaments.

BETTY BOOP

Another popular character who is produced under licence by Wade is the iconic animation film star Betty Boop. The first Wade figurine to hit the collectors' market was in 1995 and showed the figure of Betty on a green base: originally retailing at £35, it sold out instantly. Ever since this initial success the Wade pottery has continued to produce Betty Boop

figurines regularly in a variety of different poses and guises. There have also been an array of Betty in Christmas mode such as 'Christmas Morning' which shows Betty opening up her Christmas present only to find her loveable dog Pudgy popping out. Released in 2002 in a limited edition size of 750 this is one of the Christmas figures that collectors are eager to own and are willing to pay between £60 and £100 for her. Another sought after Betty Boop is the 2005 'Christmas Surprise', which was issued at the Wade Bonanza. A figure of Betty Boop dressed in a sexy Santa outfit with a sack full of presents, this particular piece is worth in the region of £100, more if you find one with the sack in a gold colour. Two more Betty Boop Christmas figures were released in 2008 at the special Christmas event, one of which was the final in the premier princess range. Dressed in her Christmas colours and wearing a lustre finished dress with green sash she was an instant hit, as was the other limited edition figurine of Betty Boop dressed in a Santa Claus outfit and entitled 'Christmas Time.'

Although Wade owns the official licence to produce ceramic Betty Boop figurines

The Wade 'Christmas Surprise' Betty Boop figurine was issued in 2005 and if found with a gold sack collectors will pay more than £100 for her.

there are also many other collectable Christmas figurines and decorations available to buy if you are a Betty Boop fan but have only a small financial budget. Many are made in resin, others can be made of glass and there are also a host of different designs. Some of the ornaments available are made purely for displaying on flat surfaces whilst others are created as Christmas tree ornaments or wall hangings. I own a few of the resin tree ornaments and whenever my friends visit they always comment on how much they love my Betty Boop Christmas decorations.

HUMMEL FIGURINES

Germany really is considered the home of Christmas and as I have already discussed many of the traditions such as Christmas trees and decorations originated from this European country. So it is no surprise that the Goebel pottery is one of the leading manufacturers of not only tree decorations but also Christmas inspired figural ornaments.

One of the most popular of the figural ornaments is the delightful ceramic statuettes of Bavarian children. First introduced in 1935 these enchanting figurines were inspired by the drawings of a nun, Sister Maria Innocentia (Berta) Hummel. Owner of the German porcelain company W Goebel Porzellanfabrik, Franz Goebel noticed Maria's work in a religious art shop and soon after created the first set of Hummel figurines which were showcased at the Leipzig Fair. An instant success these Hummel figurines continued to be made for collectors after Maria passed away in 1946 aged just thirty-seven. Each piece created after her death had to be true to Maria's original drawings and there remained a close link between the manufacturer Goebel and the Convent of Siessen where Maria had resided.

As you can imagine there have been many figures and within this a significant amount have been inspired by Christmas activities. Some of the early examples can cost collectors hundreds of pounds, whilst others are more easily acquired figurines which cost anything from £25 up to £100. One of my personal favourites is the 1980s issue of 'Ride into Christmas' which shows a boy whizzing home down the snow on a sleigh with his newly acquired Christmas tree secured in a bag behind him. This piece generally sells for around £70 to £100 and can be found on internet shop sites as well as those popular internet auctions.

Sadly at the end of 2008 it was announced by the Goebel pottery that these figurines would no longer be placed into production. This has obviously affected the collectors' market and now those older sought after figurines are becoming even harder to find as avid collectors try and track them down.

COLLECTOR'S TIP
A genuine Hummel figure always carries Berta Hummel's signature embossed on the bottom. It will also have a mould number on the base to signify it is an authentic piece. Fake figures generally do not carry the Hummel signature and are of much

poorer quality, so take time to examine a genuine figurine in order to distinguish between the real article and a badly made fake.

TUSKERS

People collect just about anything and everything and many concentrate on amassing collections of animals with some of the most popular being pigs, frogs and elephants. In 1997 Barry Price began to sculpture a range of fun, quirky elephants participating in human activities for the manufacturer Country Artists. This range has become hugely popular and over the years Barry has added many pieces to his Tuskers range which recently was taken over by Enesco.

'We Wish you an Ele Christmas' Tuskers figurine was limited to 750 pieces and it features a wonderful festive scene of three elephants messing about under the Christmas tree.

As with most collectable companies there are many Christmas themed pieces which have been released over the years. 'We wish you an Ele Christmas' is a more recent limited edition of 750 and depicts three elephants participating in various Christmas activities on a tableau base. This piece sold out more or less straight away, proving how popular these quirky, fun elephants are with collectors. Prices for Tuskers vary and can start from as little as £10 meaning that they are a great range of figural Christmas decorations for children to collect.

ROYAL DOULTON

Royal Doulton has issued so many different Christmas figurines that it is impossible to count. Some are more classical such as the collection of Christmas Day lady figurines and the more recently issued series of 'Carol Singing' figures, whilst others represent various childhood characters. The Christmas inspired collection of five Winnie the Pooh figurines consists of 'A little tree trimming is in order', 'Happy Christmas Tigger', 'The most perfect tree in the World', 'Happy Christmas Piglet', and 'Christopher dresses the tree'. This popular collection of figures not only attracts those that love Christmas but also the huge following that the loveable honey eating bear has in his own right.

When buying Royal Doulton pieces I recommend that you go for the ones that were made at the British Stoke-on-Trent pottery before its closure in 1999. Although pieces are still being made much of the production now takes place in the Far East and there is a significant difference in the actual finished product. The glazes are much more vibrant where the earlier pieces are more muted. Also collectors are more interested in those pieces that were actually made in the UK; there are, however, some collectors that started buying the pieces made in the Far East because they preferred this design.

When deciding to collect Christmas Royal Doulton pieces go for a theme rather than a mismatch of different subject matters, as this looks better when displayed. For example, many people concentrate on just collecting the lady figurines whilst others prefer the children's character collectables.

The Christmas Day lady figurines produced annually by Royal Doulton are very popular with collectors. This one is the 2006 figure and shows the elegant lady dressed in festive colours.

PETER FAGAN AND COLOURBOX

I was very honoured a few years ago to interview Peter Fagan the founder of Colourbox on behalf of one of the magazines for which I write. This interview was even more poignant for me because when I was a child I would race to the shops with my pocket money in order to buy another of his miniature ceramic resin cat ornaments. Colourbox was established in 1983 when the 'Home Sweet Home' collection was shown at the annual spring trade fair. Initially this range was mainly of cats in a variety of situations but by 1987 Peter also started to make small teddy bear figurines. Colourbox ornaments were hugely popular, especially with children, and today there are still many collectors even though Peter was forced to close Colourbox in 2000. Although Colourbox no longer exists, Peter continues to model pieces under his own name and still has a big collectors' following.

Some of the Christmas inspired pieces to look out for are 'Santa Paws' which was released in 1991 and features Father Christmas with a cat popping out from behind him. 'Mistletoe Bear' is also a lovely Christmas piece, which focuses on a teddy bear wearing a lopsided Santa hat with mistletoe in his hand, and another of my favourites is 'Christmas Pudding' which is a bear wrapped around this traditional Christmas dessert. These wonderful ornaments are so affordable and can be picked up for a few pounds; they look great as a collection on the fireplace and once again are perfect for children to source and collect.

The 1991 Colourbox Christmas figure by Peter Fagan was entitled 'Santa Paws' and featured a cheeky black cat peering out from behind Santa.

'Mistletoe Bear' is another example of the Christmas pieces created by Peter Fagan for Colourbox.

BORDER FINE ARTS

The Scottish company Border Fine Arts was founded by John Hammond in 1974 and today is classed as a leading manufacturer of sculptural figurines. Boasting many talented designers and modellers the subject matters are mainly based on country living and agricultural farming. Some collectors are prepared to pay hundreds even thousands of pounds to own some of the rare and early pieces, especially if sculpted by Anne Wall or Ray Ayres (who celebrated his thirtieth anniversary with the company in 2006).

Aside from these farming scenes and wildlife studies Border Fine Arts also holds the licence to produce collectable figurines of Beatrix Potter, Brambly Hedge and Winnie the Pooh. These sculptural character collectables form part of their studio range and are increasing in popularity all the time.

Jill Barklem's series of books *Brambly Hedge* is probably my most favourite of the Border Fine Arts pieces. The delightful characters such as Wilfred Toadflax, Dusty Dogwood and Poppy Eyebright have been recreated into some of the most exciting sculptural tableau settings and figurines. One of the Christmas pieces that I adore most is that of the limited edition tableau 'Merry Winter' designed by Richard Wawrzesta and features Primrose and Wilfred entertaining Lord and Lady Woodmouse at Christmas. A piece that conjures up images of how a traditional Christmas should be celebrated I think this particular Christmas collectable appeals to all those that adore the festive season as much as I do.

JIM SHORE

Up until a few months ago I was oblivious to the vibrant coloured designs of award-winning artist Jim Shore. Whist standing in a department store his collection of Disney themed Christmas collectable figural ornaments caught my eye and I was instantly drawn. On further research I discovered that these pieces are inspired by traditional American folklore and his designs are taken from wonderful antique quilting patterns, appliqué work and rose malling which is a form of decorative painting which features swirls and circles. In 2000 Jim began his collaboration with Enesco and since has won many prestigious awards including Christmas Collectable of the year in 2003 and 2005 and also Christmas Décor of the year in 2004 and 2005.

All Shore's creations are made from stone resin (polyresin) and are highly decorative making them the ideal Christmas ornament. Shore has produced a whole host of various Christmas ornaments, which include Father Christmas, reindeers and angels as well as a set of more traditional-looking carol singers. However, the range that I think is most appealing to collectors is that of the Disney Christmas ornaments. From Mickey Mouse to Goofy and Tinker Bell to Winnie the Pooh all our favourite characters have been recreated in Jim Shore's unique style, not only making them wonderful ornaments to display around the home but also the ideal gift for any Disney enthusiast.

Jim Shore produces wonderful Christmas designs inspired by traditional folklore, quilting patterns and appliqué work. He also has produced a host of Disney inspired Christmas pieces in the same colourful designs like this piece 'A Christmas Kiss' with Mickey and Minnie Mouse.

ALESSI

I know you might find this a bit strange as the Italian design company Alessi are generally known for their kitchen and household products rather than Christmas decorations but a few months ago whilst on holiday in Italy I discovered that they had indeed released a range of decorations.

The other appealing quality is that each of the porcelain decorations is slightly quirky

The Italian design company Alessi have also recently released some fantastic arty Christmas figural ornaments including the porcelain 'Christmas Cowboy Figurine' which costs around £20 and would make an unusual quirky display.

off-the-wall designs such as the 'Christmas Cowboy Figurine', which features a large reindeer being ridden by Father Christmas and retails at around £20. There are also a few others in the collection, which have all been designed by Massimo Giacon and include a bizarre modernist-style nativity scene entitled 'Christmas Presepe Group Figurines' and the 'Christmas Natalino Figurine', which is of Father Christmas leaning up against a white and green flecked Christmas tree.

   Not only are these affordable decorations but they are also very much in keeping with the Alessi element of design. Something totally different that will appeal to those who prefer a more modern Christmas these quirky innovative decorations are a definite talking piece when your friends and family come visiting.

DELECTABLE DECORATIONS

There is such an assortment of items available with which to decorate your home at Christmas that it is difficult to know where to start and in all honesty . . . where to end. I have only mentioned the figural and ornamental ones that I have around the house during the festive period but am sure many of you have hundreds of other suggestions. The key thing to Christmas decorations is to make sure that you display them in a way that gives you pleasure, maybe some of those ornaments only come out in the run up to Christmas but perhaps you have a collection that is on display all year around. Whatever your preference, and however you decorate, as long as the end result is a warm Christmas glow then you have achieved the desired effect which makes this time of year so welcoming.

TOP TIPS FOR COLLECTING CHRISTMAS ORNAMENTS

- Look for items that are available for the Christmas period only.
- The smaller the limited edition sizes the more collectable.
- Source Christmas collectable ornaments which are advertised in magazines and newspapers as most of these can only be bought through this forum and not readily available in the shops.
- Purchase those items made exclusively for certain retail outlets and not available through any other stores.
- Buy items that are not only associated with Christmas but also crossover into other collecting categories such as advertising memorabilia or nostalgic television characters as this widens their collectable appeal.
- Buy good quality, well-known factory or designer named items that will continue in popularity.
- Keep the Christmas packaging as this too can become collectable in its own right.
- Make sure that any receipts, boxes or paraphernalia is also stored away in order to add future collectability.
- If looking to buy out of production items **DO** research first to make sure you buy at the cheapest and best price from reputable dealers.

- Always buy from reputable dealers who can confirm that a product is genuine.
- Buy older pieces out of season as Christmas collectable figures and ornaments tend to shoot up in price in the run up to Christmas then drop again once the festive celebrations are over.

CHAPTER 6

NATIVITY COLLECTABLES

Another decoration that can be found displayed in some people's homes is the long-standing tradition of the Nativity. Not quite as popular as in past decades this traditional scene seems to have fallen out of fashion but is still very much an integral part of Christmas celebrations. This figural scene is a retelling of the story of the birth of Jesus as written in the bible from the gospel of Luke and Matthew. The custom of displaying a nativity in the home as a decoration originates from Germany during the 1600s. This decorative religious scene generally consists of Mary, Joseph, the manger (cradle or crib) with baby Jesus inside, the three wise men, shepherds and various animals such as the donkey or ox with the angel Gabriel looking down and sometimes the star of Bethlehem at the top of a stable or cave.

HISTORY OF THE NATIVITY DECORATION

FACT
St Francis of Assisi asked for permission from Pope Honorius III to celebrate the birth of Christ in his own way as nativity dramas had been banned. In 1223 he put on a simple show in a cave where a manger was set up along with an ox and donkey. The manger was the altar to which St Francis gave Christmas mass. Although not the traditional nativity with kings and shepherds still very much a celebration of the birth of Jesus Christ.

In the Seventeenth Century German artisans began to carve nativity figures from wood so that they could be displayed in churches, homes and markets. This was also the case in Italy although the materials used depended on the region. For example in Sicily mother of pearl and alabaster were the favoured materials whilst in Naples the figures were created from wood and terracotta. The designs from Naples were also carved and sculptured by leading artists of the time and were mainly produced for the rich to display in their homes. Much more elaborate and dramatic, these figures also showcased the artist's capabilities and talents.

By the Eighteenth Century the nativity scene started to popularise around the world with not just carved figures but whole nativity scenes showing the figures displayed in stables and caves. It has also for many centuries been recreated in pictorial form on murals, stained glass windows and paintings. Today the nativity is synonymous with Christmas and the birth of the baby Jesus meaning that there is a wealth of different designs available to choose from.

FACT
The Nativity Scene is also known as the Christmas Crib, in France the Nativity Crèche, in Germany the Krippe, in Italy it's presepio and in Spain it is the nacimiento.

Over the years many leading manufacturers have reproduced their own nativity scenes which are available in a variety of different forms and materials. Some are made from ceramic whilst others are resin, plastic, chalk, bronze or even glass. Many are cleverly sculptured whilst others are more simplistic and aimed at children. However, nearly all have become collectable and so fit nicely into the category of Christmas collectables.

COLLECTING NATIVITY SCENES

There are so many varied types of nativity scenes that it really is difficult to know where to start. There are those that are more traditional looking as well as modern designed nativity

Nativity scenes have been made in every material imaginable with this modern resin nativity being an example of the range of scenes that can be found.

Peter Fagan produced a sweet little ceramic nativity featuring mice and called 'Pennywhistle Lane Nativity'.

scenes and even high art for the more contemporary home. Some have been blown in glass whilst others have been produced in toy form for children to assemble and play with. There are even sets that have been made from leather and others, which take on a more quirky look by being wrapped around a Christmas tree ornament. So unless you already know exactly what type of nativity you would like to collect the choice can be quite daunting.

VINTAGE SCENES

When I say vintage I am referring to those dating from the 1950s onwards as these are still quite easy to find. Many nativity scenes from this era were manufactured either in Japan, Germany or Italy. Hard plastic was a popular material, as was papier mâché and resin. Some companies also made the animals with woollen bodies and wood stick legs whilst others produced items in hard plastic that resembled ivory. Today you can pay anything from £15 depending on whether they are individual nativity figures or a more basic moulded plastic ornament which were often given as gifts to children.

Within all avenues of collecting there are always rare items to be found and this is also the case with nativity scenes. The toy manufacturer Britains who is better known for producing hollow die-cast military figures has also produced some Christmas pieces. The nativity scene 'Herald H5320' dates to 1958/59 and was packaged in a dark blue conical-shaped box which was decorated with gold star details. In 2006, an excellent example in fantastic condition came up for sale at Vectis Auctioneers and realised £460.

Nativity scenes dating from the 1950s onwards were often made of hard plastic making them more affordable for people to buy then and collectors to acquire now.

FACT
The 1950 issue of the *Radio Times* magazine featured a nativity scene on the front cover by illustrator and author Walter Hodges.

PORCELAIN AND CERAMIC NATIVITY SCENES

Today there are far more elaborate nativity scenes available for Christmas display as nearly every manufacturer has produced one. From Lladro to Royal Doulton and Goebel to Wade there are nativity scenes somewhere in the factory archives. A seasonal subject that is much in demand, the ceramics and porcelain industries have ensured that they too produce something that not only looks the part in the home at Christmas but also adds value to give a collectable appeal.

Lladro have produced some of the most exquisite nativity scenes however they are also

The rare Britains' nativity scene with hollow die-cast figures entitled 'Herald H5320' in original conical-shaped packaging.

some of the most expensive sets to acquire. This porcelain sculptural company have produced many different nativity figures and sets over the years and you can choose between glazed or matt finish, with some of the pieces also having the option of being used as Christmas tree decorations as well as normal stand alone ornaments. You can also purchase the stable separately, but this does tend to be quite a pricey collectable with many of them costing hundreds of pounds. The figures also sell for over £100 or more each depending on how rare they are. So if you wanted a complete set of Lladro nativity figures with stable you could expect to pay over £1,000 (perhaps nearer to £2,000) so this set really is only for the serious collector.

However, don't despair if a Lladro nativity is what you would love to own; one particular scene to keep an eye out for is the 'Mini Holy Family' which was only produced during 1989 and was sculptured by Francisco Polope. Consisting of just Joseph, Mary and the baby Jesus this set is much cheaper, I have seen it sell for around £30 to £50.

Royal Doulton have also contributed their skills to producing nativity scenes and one of

Over the years Lladro have produced many different nativity scenes and figures so there is much to choose from.

the nicest, in my opinion, is the very modern porcelain set from their 'Holiday Traditions' collection. A colourful and very traditional looking ornamental nativity scene decorated with gold accents this is priced at a more realistic £100 to £150 if you include both the traditional nativity figures and the additional set which comprises of the three kings and a shepherd.

Since the 1950s the German manufacturer Goebel have released figural variations to the nativity scene, some being plain white porcelain and others more colourful. One set in particular which doesn't necessarily make the connection of being a traditional nativity scene figure but is still very desirable is a 'Flight into Egypt'. Released in 1959 this set depicts Mary on a donkey with the baby Jesus being led by a separate figure of Joseph with a lantern.

The Hummel range produced by the Goebel pottery has also released nativity figures in the form of their collectable Bavarian children. Mary is amongst one of the most prized items as is the wooden stable made to house these figures. Another set released in 1951 consists of sixteen figures including Mary mother of God, good old Saint Joseph bearing fruit, sweet infant Jesus, holy angel, wise men kneeling shepherd boy, and animals such as a camel and calf. Again this is an expensive set to buy priced in the region of £900 to £1000 because it is so scarce.

If you prefer the contemporary look to the more traditional colourful scenes then Wade have produced nativity figures that would suit the more minimalist home. Finished in white glaze with gold accents there are two modern issued sets to choose from. The first consists of the three kings, shepherd, angel and the holy family, however a second set 'Donkey, Frankincense and Myrrh' is also available to enhance this collection.

Another favourite collectable series from the Wade pottery is their extensive selection of Whimsie miniatures. In 2007 Wade also added a set of the nativity scene to their

The Wade nativity set was released in white glaze with gold accents so would suit a more minimalist home.

This Wade Whimsie nativity scene is a favourite collectable.

Whimsie collection and these six figures are a must-have for any collector of Christmas ornaments.

In fact, if your preferred area of collecting is miniature items another nativity scene to seek out is the bone china example made by Hagen Renaker. First introduced in the autumn of 1991 it was designed by Robert McGuinness. When it was first released there were six figures in the series, Mary, Joseph, baby Jesus and the three wise men. Shortly afterwards additional pieces were added such as the camel, a grey donkey with purple blanket, ewe and lamb. There has also been a shepherd boy with lamb, shepherd with crook, and two angels. The first angel was issued with gold wings and the second with white wings. Then of course you can't have a nativity scene without a manger and that was originally released in 1991.

Fact
Hagen Renaker was established in 1945 by John and Maxine Renaker from their garage in Culver City, America. Their first kiln was a garden hose running from their gas oven.

GLASS NATIVITY SCENES

Although there are a large variety of different porcelain, ceramic and bone china examples available to collectors there are also many other nativity scenes to find that are made from glass. The French crystal glass-maker Baccarat resides at the high end of the collectable market as their nativity figure can cost anything from £200 and more. Delicate figures care has to be taken as they are easily broken or chipped. Waterford Crystal and the American company Gorham Crystal also produce a range of various nativity figures and each of these are in a more affordable price bracket. However, the quality is not in the same league as that of Baccarat although they still produce the desired effect when displayed.

COLLECTOR'S FACT
Instead of a label, in 1936 Baccarat started to sign their works with an acid or sandblasted mark.

FUN AND QUIRKY ALTERNATIVES

Aside from the more traditional scenes available to collectors there is also an array of fun collectable nativity sets. The giftware manufacturers of Cherished Teddies have released many Christmas inspired figures since they began in 1992, with their early teddies being the most sought after. They have also produced music boxes based on the Nativity with the rarest being a revolving piece where the lamb moves around the nativity crèche to the music of Silent Night. This particular piece was introduced in 1993 and ceased production in 1994, and I have seen it for sale at a staggering £200. However, an alternative musical Cherished Teddies nativity scene entitled 'O Little Town of Bethlehem' can be bought at a more reasonable £30 to £40.

Another fun but slightly more adult version of the Nativity which must not be taken too seriously was produced by the 'Bad Taste Bears Company'. Not to everyone's taste, but certainly amusing, they released a few ranges inspired by the traditional nativity scene. One in particular is of Joseph pointing accusingly at the baby in the crib and Mary holding her hands up as if to say 'I don't know how he got here!' The 'While Shepherds Watched' was the third set released in 2006 and is slightly more rude but when all the collection is placed within the stable I can guarantee it will raise a laugh from your visitors.

Cherished Teddies have produced many Christmas inspired figures including this fun nativity scene.

CHILDREN'S NATIVITY SCENES

Nativity scenes and figures are also available that appeal to children. In 1958 the toy manufacturer Ideal produced a baby Jesus doll. Made of vinyl he was presented in a book-shaped box entitled 'The Most Wonderful Story'. This box had wonderful colourful text and included stand-up card figures which gave the impression of the main nativity figures standing and kneeling around the doll itself. Today this doll is not easy to find but is the perfect reminder of why we celebrate this festive period.

More recently Ashton Drake released a twenty-one-inch baby doll complete with wooden manger filled with straw. This incredibly lifelike doll is aptly called 'Away in a Manger' and is made of soft touch vinyl. Designed by Waltraud Hanl he is already very collectable.

A rare nativity doll is the one produced by Ideal in 1958. Made of vinyl he was presented in a wonderful box-shaped like a book.

More recently Ashton Drake released a lifelike nativity baby Jesus doll which is already very collectable.

The German teddy bear and soft toy manufacturer Steiff have also realised the collectability of the nativity and in 2005 launched the first of three nativity inspired scenes. This initial collection was a sell-out success and featured two small mohair teddy bears dressed as Mary and Joseph, a baby teddy bear in the crib and an ox and donkey. Because this scene was such a hit with collectors in 2006 another set followed of a teddy bear shepherd dressed in linen and a waistcoat, along with his shepherd boy son, a billy goat and two lambs. 2007 saw the three wise men join the nativity and each of these mohair bears are dressed in

The initial 2005 Steiff nativity manger scene was a sell-out success and today is a prized piece with collectors of both Christmas memorabilia and those that adore bears.

Never ignore the unmarked nativity scenes available on the market, this ceramic version belongs to my friend and I think it is extremely stylish.

elaborate rich clothing and includes a regal looking camel. Now all three collections are very desirable with both collectors of nativity scenes as well as teddy bear enthusiasts.

If dolls and bears don't appeal then there are also nativity toys for the boys. Playmobil have issued two assembly kits, one being the 'Nativity Manger' and the other 'Three Wise Kings'. Both include the famed Playmobil plastic figures and animals with accessories as well as a cardboard backdrop and a copy of the Christmas story to help children understand the importance of this event. Playmobil already has a huge following with adult collectors and these nativity sets are sure to ignite the collecting passion in children, as well as teach them about the true meaning of Christmas.

Nativity Scenes have also appeared in snow globe form which adds an extra sparkle to this tradition decoration.

DECORATIVE VALUE ONLY

Aside from all the named manufactured nativity scenes there are absolutely hundreds that are unmarked and available from shops throughout the run up to Christmas. Just because these don't necessarily have a collectable following doesn't mean that they are not worth buying. My mum has a passion for nativity scenes and she came round to my home very excited last Christmas carrying her latest buy. It was an unusual wood-carved one-piece standing nativity scene inlaid with small pieces of mirrored glass. She had paid £30 and although it doesn't have collectable appeal it is still an unusual nativity scene I know she will display with pride. My friend also owns one of the most stylish unmarked ceramic nativities that I have ever seen. So when next out shopping please don't ignore the masses of different nativity crib scenes available to buy as these were made to be displayed and enjoyed.

CHAPTER 7

SNOW GLOBES

A SNOWSTORM OF A CHRISTMAS

It is always strange when suddenly you are confronted with an item that jolts you back to reliving those childhood memories and this is exactly what happened when I began to write this book. Until I started to research Christmas and the items surrounding it I had almost forgotten about the enchanting snow globes which would appear every year either in my Christmas stocking or as a decorative ornament on the fireplace. These older ones from my childhood years in the 1970s would form hours of entertainment as I would either shake them to make the snow fall or just fantasise about the theme encased within the clear plastic dome. An integral part of Christmas I could not write this book without at least mentioning a little about this tradition and so I began to delve deeper into why the snow globe exists and has become another of those wonderful Christmas collectables.

A collection of vintage snow globes depicting a variety of different scenes.

HISTORY OF THE SNOW GLOBE

The very first snow globes appeared around the Victorian era and were originally used as paperweights. Made of glass they contained a variety of materials such as porcelain, china chips, metal flakes, bone fragments or ground rice which gave the impression of falling snow when the glass was shaken. The liquid inside was originally just water but later glycol was added in order to slow the fall of the snow thus giving the impression of a gently falling snow flurry. Of course no snow globe is complete without a scene inside and quite often the main focus point is of a figure or animal which will get covered in snow when the globe is shaken. Many of the globes were originally created as tourist pieces and the Victorians would collect these souvenirs to take home as a reminder of their travels. Novelty items were popular during this time and at the 1878 Paris 'all nations' Exhibition there was a display of snow globes available for the public to view. Avid collectors eagerly seek these early French examples today, especially if they are able to secure those with porcelain or marble bases.

Another factory renowned for producing snow globes is that of The Erwin Perzy factory based in Vienna. They manufactured these globes from 1900 and are known for their simplistic style which features fine hand painted details. They also used a liquid substance which allowed the snow to suspend in the air for over a minute before settling.

By the 1920s and 30s snow globes came into their own and proved popular as novelty gifts and decorations. This is also the time when snow globes filtered over to America, gaining instant popularity. Atlas Crystal Works were the main manufacturers having factories both in the States and Germany and even today the Americans are among the largest collectors of both modern and vintage snow globes.

However, it was the German manufacturer Koziol who came up with the idea of producing an oval globe in 1948 as they believed that this shape would be more difficult to break. It also meant that this new shape could have a flat coloured backing and, whereas before the scene could be viewed three-dimensionally, now the figures could only be viewed from the front so there was no need for three-dimensional characters to be placed inside. This new initiative also helped saved on labour and realised the snow globe shape that is known today. This manufacturer is still producing snow globes using the traditional techniques and original moulds that they have always used.

Collector's Fact
The liquid in the majority of snow globes will gradually evaporate and sometimes change colour.

By the 1950s and 60s it was commonplace for all children to find a snow globe tucked into their Christmas stocking. These would feature festive scenes and seasonal characters such as angels, reindeers or Father Christmas and would supply endless hours of fun for the recipients.

Earlier domes were made of glass but it was around the 1950s that they started to be produced in plastic. Although most collectors crave the earlier glass domes the plastic ones are also desirable. Available with all kinds of different scenes, some were still manufactured so that you could see the scene all the way around the globe (like the one I picked up recently from a table sale) but others had the flat back. The best thing about collecting snow globes from the 1950s onwards is that they are affordable on the pocket. The one I bought cost only 20p but generally you should expect to spend a few pounds on good examples of vintage snow globes. Much older ones, made of glass and which date back to the Victorian period, will cost much more depending on the condition. Rare ones can set you back as much as £100 or more but these are few and far between as few survived.

Collector's Fact
Look for those snow globes made of glass with wood, Bakelite, or ceramic bases as these are more sought after by collectors.

Around the 1950s snow globes started to be made from plastic and today these examples can be picked up for pennies, thus making a wonderful affordable collection.

Modern Globes

Today snow globes are far more sophisticated; they tend to be filled with plastic snow rather than the earlier primitive materials. Many feature glitter, stars or coloured beads as their falling snow whilst others contain polystyrene. The mechanics behind the modern snow globe have also changed; some have musical mechanisms placed into the bottom whilst others feature handles that you turn to get the snow going rather than using the more traditional technique of actually shaking the globe. They still however, give the desired effect and some of the modern versions are highly collected.

Although originally these snow globes were associated with Christmas and tourist souvenirs today they are available with an array of different subject matters. You can still buy them easily from seaside shops as a way of remembering your holiday, much like in the Victorian days but you can also find them in many gift shops with different collectable scenes.

Beware
Some manufacturers inject anti-freeze into the snow globe liquid
to stop them from freezing during shipping – this is harmful to
small children and pets so keep them out of reach.

Look for Disney snow globes as these are highly sought after with collectors, especially if they have a musical mechanism or have features outside of the globe.

Collectable Globes

Disney

Disney is a popular subject matter and many of the scenes from the films are found in different globes. Some of the Disney ones can become extremely sought after and recently I saw a modern musical Disney 'Little April Shower' globe, which featured three-dimensional figures mounted on the outside of the globe with a figure of Bambi inside the glass dome, sell for a staggering £120. In fact, many of the musical Disney modern globes all tend to sell for over £60 each and the more work to the outside of a globe, the more money they can command.

The Snowman

The ceramics manufacturer Coalport has released glass snow globes featuring Raymond Brigg's popular character The Snowman. Better known as 'Glitter Globes' one of the most collected from this range is 'Treading the Boards' which shows the Snowman and James dancing. Another one released by Coalport features the Snowman giving James a hug but yet one of the hardest to find is a special which was released for the 'Snowman Guild' of collectors and is entitled 'At the Party'. This particular globe can sell for £40 or more.

Me to You Bears

First created in 1997 by Carte Blanche Greetings Ltd, Me to You Bears (also known as Tatty Bears) are highly collected and they too have been reproduced within snow globes. Again there is a variety to choose from; some are very basic and have just one bear inside with a pale blue or pink base, others are larger and may house two bears, but recently the globes have become more ornate. In 2008 'Up, Up and Away' was released for the Christmas market. This globe depicted a Christmas scene of reindeer pulling a sleigh being driven off of the roof of a house, with a clear globe in the middle which had the driver (Santa Me to You Bear) encased within. These were retailing at £60 each from all major stores.

General Snow Globes

Aside from the commercial collectable globes there is also an abundance of different shapes, sizes and designs in more standard Christmas globes. Some feature the globe with a scene inside, others have an external appearance with either a snowman or Father Christmas wrapped around the globe. Generally these are made of plastic and cost a few pounds to buy as additional Christmas decorations but can cost more if made of glass. The trick to looking for globes that will become collectable is to buy quality. Although cheap plastic 1950s globes are highly desirable some of the modern ones may not become quite as sought after, however if they are innovative enough, made to a standard, and feature an unusual design they are sure to become the collectables of the future, so don't dismiss these cheaper options when hunting around the shops.

FACT
Several stores sell small, cheap snow globes, which are made with very thin glass. They shatter extremely easily, sometimes even if just held tightly. So parents with young children should beware of cheap snow globes, and buy only from a reputable stockist.

Nativity scenes are a popular feature encased inside a
snow globe and make lovely decorative ornaments.

FILMS FEATURING SNOW GLOBES

Many films and television programmes have featured snow globes within the scenes. The 1937 film *Heidi* staring Shirley Temple showed a little girl peering into a snow shaker of a miniature cabin, and then there was the dramatic scene from the 1939 film *Citizen Kane* where the dying Charles Foster Kane drops a snow globe on the floor. The American series *St Elsewhere* has also featured this Christmas icon when the father of an autistic son places a globe on top of the television, leading you to believe that the *St Elsewhere* saga was simply a figment of the boy's imagination.

DISPLAY YOUR COLLECTION

If you intend or already have a healthy collection of snow globes then they look best if displayed together. Try and keep them in a cabinet or on a sturdy shelf so that they won't become broken. You will be surprised how the wonderful colours and shapes when placed together make a stunning display especially if you are able to artificially light them.

Top Tips For Looking after Your Snow Globes

- Make sure you store your snow globe away properly by wrapping in bubble wrap as they are easily broken and almost impossible to mend.
- It is a possibility that globes can freeze so make sure they are kept at a stable temperature.
- As with any collectable sunlight can be damaging so keep the globes out of direct sunlight to stop the possibility of fading.
- Heat is also dangerous as these glass globes can easily ignite as they act like a magnifying glass. So keep them away from direct sunlight or heat that could set them on fire.
- Algae can form within the water if they have too much light on the globes.
- Only wipe them over with a damp cloth to clean as abrasive cleaning products can damage them easily.

NOSTALGIC QUALITIES

Snow globes are, in my opinion, one of the most memorable of Christmas collectables. These simplistic glass or plastic domes have kept children and adults amused for well over 100 years and even today it is impossible for anyone to walk past a globe in a shop or on a fireplace without giving it a good shake. The other appealing thing about collecting snow globes is that they can be acquired reasonably cheaply, so there is no need to spend a fortune amassing a collection. This is also a great way to start children on the road to collecting, or alternatively a way of revisiting an adult's nostalgic happy memories. Snow globes have become one of my favourites within the Christmas collecting circuit and I will now definitely make sure that a few find their way into my friend's Christmas stockings in the hope that these too will recapture their childhood memories.

CHAPTER 8

COLLECTABLE CHRISTMAS CARDS

For me, sending Christmas cards out to all my friends and family is a bit of a chore. I generally forget someone, or write the card then never actually post it so after Christmas I find a sealed white envelope with someone's name on under the tree. However, I do love buying the cards. There are so many to choose from that I usually end up spending a fortune on loads of boxes as I cannot decide which ones I want. There are those with festive winter scenes, others depict playful children or animals, many are humorous with Santa getting stuck in the chimney, or there are even now really modern selections with images of fashion items or vintage toys. The choice is endless but this wasn't always a Christmas tradition and there were certainly never as many designs to pick from as there are today.

THE FIRST EVER CHRISTMAS CARD

We have Sir Henry Cole to thank for first coming up with the idea of a Christmas card. It was common place during the early Nineteenth Century for people to write seasonal

The Christmas card was invented by Henry Cole and illustrated by John Callcott-Horsley. In 2001 Henry Aldridge and Sons Auctions made the record price by selling this card signed by Cole for a staggering £22,500.

messages inside letters or on their calling cards but in 1843, in order to save himself from writing dozens of messages, Henry Cole came up with the innovative idea of printing seasonal cards which had the message 'A Merry Christmas and A Happy New Year' already printed inside.

ABOUT HENRY

Henry Cole was one of the most important figures of the Nineteenth Century. Originally he started work at the age of fifteen for the Public Records Office where he was instrumental in reforming the company and preserving the national archives. After leaving employment with the records office he began to work as an assistant to Rowland Hill who was the main campaigner for the reform of the postal system and was responsible for introducing the penny postage system. Henry Cole was an important part of this campaign and was also instrumental in introducing the world's first ever adhesive stamp, the Penny Black. Cole is also said to have been the man responsible for designing this stamp, which features the profile of Queen Victoria's head.

Cole also had an interest in the arts and especially industrial design. A member of the Society for the Encouragement of Arts, Manufactures, and Commerce, Cole campaigned to improve the standards in industrial design. He secured the backing from Queen Victoria's husband, Prince Albert, and in 1847 the Society was granted a royal charter. Cole went on to organise the Exhibition of Art in 1847, which proved so successful that in 1848 and 1849 he organised even bigger exhibitions. Cole was also responsible for opening up the exhibitions to the international market after he had visited the Paris Exhibition in 1849. With the backing of Queen Victoria, the Royal Commission for the Exhibition of 1851 was established with Prince Albert as the President. Entitled 'The Great Exhibition of the Worlds of Industry of all Nations', it was a massive success both financially and popularly. This massive exhibition is probably one of the most famous of its time and was held at Crystal Palace in Hyde Park, London.

After the success of the exhibition (mostly due to the management skills of Henry Cole) £186,000 was used to improve the education of science and art. Some land was purchased in the South Kensington area of London and was developed into educational institutions. Cole was then made General Superintendent of the Department of Practical Art and it was through this posting that he was able to begin the development of the famous Victoria and Albert Museum. Cole was made the first Director and today this museum still is the most prestigious for art and industrial design.

FACT
Henry Cole was awarded the CB (companion) for his work on the Great Exhibition, and in 1875 was knighted by Queen Victoria.

COLE'S CHRISTMAS CARD

When Cole first decided he wanted to create a Christmas greeting card he approached his friend John Callcott-Horsley who was already a well-established and reputable artist. Callcott-Horsley illustrated the front of the card, which depicted a panel to either side each featuring two acts of charity; 'feeding the hungry' and 'clothing the naked'. The centre featured three generations of a well off family happily drinking and celebrating Christmas. However this illustrative design did cause some controversy as one of the family drinking was a small child and this was not well received by the public at first.

The card itself was lithograph printed by Jobbins of Warrick Court in London on stiff cardboard and measured approximately five inches by three inches inside. It was professionally hand-coloured by a man named Mason and 1,000 were printed. Henry Cole took the amount he needed to send out to his friends and relatives and then sold the remaining cards in London for one shilling each, a price that only the wealthy could afford.

Today this first ever Christmas card is extremely sought after by collectors and as very few remain (supposedly only ten are known to exist) there is strong competition to own one. Usually if these genuine Victorian Henry Cole cards turn up at auction they reach around £6,000 to £8,000. However in November 2001 an extremely valuable card went up for sale at Henry Aldridge & Son Auctioneers in Devizes, Wiltshire. It was unique in the fact that this particular version of the card was personally signed by Henry Cole as he had sent it to his 'Granny and Auntie Char'– when it was sold it achieved a staggering £22,500 which stands as the world record price for the first ever Christmas card.

> One of the most avid collectors of Victorian Christmas cards was Queen Mary. Her collection was displayed in a large selection of albums and is today housed in the British Museum in London.

MASS PRODUCTION CARDS

Once the Cole Christmas card had debuted, like any other successful idea, others started to produce their own cards. The following year saw various artists and illustrators bring out their designs and sell them as seasonal cards as this gave them further work opportunities. Artists would design the front of the cards whilst the writers would come up with poems or slogans to go inside. Famous artists such as Kate Greenaway and Thomas Crane illustrated their art on the front of cards and companies even offered prizes for the most artistic designs. Companies trying to find the right poems and suitable sentiments would spend thousands of pounds.

FACT
One of the biggest collectors of Christmas cards was a gentleman named Jonathon King who turned his Islington house into a museum. In the 1890s his collection consisted of around 163,000 different cards dating from 1862 to 1895, which weighed up to seven tons. The whole collection was destroyed in 1918 by a house fire.

Early Designs

The early cards would not depict the religious or winter scenes that are often found on our cards today, instead they favoured fairies, flowers and fanciful designs associated with the winter season coming to an end and celebrating the approaching spring. These Victorian-era cards were very much about opulence and good living. Some were heavily embossed whilst others possessed iridescent designs. Many had decorative piercing whilst others featured humorous images. They were also available in an array of different shapes such as oval and crescent, and some were even shaped like bells or shoes. Mostly elaborate in design these cards were incredibly innovative as they appeared in folded form or even in some cases needed turning upside down to reveal the message, poem or verse inside.

With so many different manufacturers there were many variations in cards with each of the publishing houses trying to produce something different to the next. Collectors tend to look for the most innovative designs or those that epitomise the era but some prefer to just source certain publishers.

Many Victorian cards had elaborate fanciful designs like this early example featuring birds sitting on a garden fence with exquisite piercing work.

Benjamin Sulman

London based lithograph printer Benjamin Sulman is renowned for both his Christmas and Valentine cards. His company was to lead the way forward for commercialising Christmas and his cards were considerably more ambitious than others on the market. They featured cards which were engraved, embossed and die stamped with some even more adventurous with lace edging.

Look for the B Sulman London Trademark stamp when sourcing cards from this period.

Goodall & Son

However, the Christmas card as we know it today didn't start until later when a British publisher, Goodall & Son, embarked on the first mass-production run. They had been

producing Christmas stationery since the late 1850s; however in 1866 Mr Josiah Goodall commissioned Marcus Ward & Co. to lithograph a set of four different designs which had been drawn by the artist C H Bennett. The following year the company again commissioned the artist to design cards and along with festive borders drawn by Luke Limner of robins, mistletoe and holly these first mass-produced cards set the precedent for the Christmas cards that we know and love today.

Goodall cards feature a heart trademark.

De La Rue & Co.

Famous for producing stamps, playing cards and bank notes De La Rue & Co. was established in 1835. They began producing Christmas cards in 1872 and are probably most renowned for the cards bearing images of nude children. They ceased production of cards in 1885.

A De La Rue & Co. Christmas card showing the image of a nude girl.

Marcus Ward & Co.

Originally established in Belfast, Ireland, Marcus Ward & Co. was a colour printing and publishing business. In 1867 they were so successful that the company was able to set up offices in London, which is where they became renowned for high quality decorative excellence in festive cards. Their designs featured lithographed gold borders and employed some of the best-known illustrators of the time such as Kate Greenaway who began working with them from 1871. In fact it was this Christmas card work that brought Greenaway into the public eye as her unusual talent of drawing young children appealed to the Victorian sentiment. Today, if you managed to find an original Greenaway Christmas card you can pay up to as much as £500 for it, depending on the subject matter and condition.

Sadly by the 1880s Marcus Ward & Co. began to import cheap German products for their cards. This demise in quality meant that the public lost faith in their cards and by the mid 1890s the company was struggling to survive. In 1899 Marcus Ward & Co. had gone into dissolution and it was their rival company M'Caw, Stevenson & Orr who agreed with the liquidators in 1900 to purchase the entire business.

Eyre & Spottiswoode

Printers to the Queen, George Edward Eyre and William Spottiswoode began printing Christmas cards from 1878. These cards featured unusual figural work and were classed as being both elegant and tasteful.

Raphael Tuck

Born in East Prussia in 1821, Raphael Tuck moved to England in 1865 and set up a shop which sold pictures and framing. By 1870 his three brothers had joined the company and together they ventured into the world of publishing, manufacturing their first Christmas card in 1871. During 1880 Raphael Tuck came up with the idea of launching a competition to find originality in design for Christmas cards. Thousands of images were entered from various sources and the company gave away massive cash prizes for the best.

Raphael Tuck continued to be a success until 1940 when its premises were destroyed by fire during one of the biggest air raids in the Second World War. Their entire archives were lost.

Alfred Bryan

This designer is best known for his illustrations of political cartoons on cards. He designed the famous Gladstone in an express train illustration and the even better known card of Lord Randolph Churchill (Winston Churchill's father) sitting on a crescent moon playing the mandolin.

SOME OF THE OTHER CHRISTMAS CARDS AND MANUFACTURERS

Wolff Hagelberg – Contains pictures of angels watching over children, novelty designs, and one of a Punch and Judy show which when held to the light showed the image in silhouette.

Walter Crane – Political cards.

S. Hildersheimer & Co. – Produced a set of cards called 'The Penny Basket'.

Angus Thomas – Designed the famous 'Ode to the Specials' card which was created after the 'Bloody Sunday' demonstrations held in Trafalgar Square on 13 November 1887.

Hermin Rothe – Unusually designed cards depicting slightly off-the-wall images such as a potato dressed as a gent. These cards were manufactured from 1874 to 1890s.

COLLECTING VICTORIAN CHRISTMAS CARDS

During the Victorian era there were many variations of designs and styles available throughout the festive period. They included everything from religious scenes through to

This elaborate Victorian Christmas card featuring lanterns has pierced work and when held up to the light it glows through the lanterns.

daily Victorian life and one of the most popular themes was that of nudity. When it comes to collecting these early cards of course we would all love to own the rare examples, but thankfully there are many other general cards available. Price depends on the card's manufacturer, its age, subject matter, and of course condition. Expect to pay in the region of £35 to £50 for those depicting a popular theme such as Punch and Judy, alternatively those that epitomise Victoriana can sell for a similar amount. Generally though, normal standard Victorian Christmas cards can be picked up from as little as a few pounds, increasing to around £25. However the ones bearing manufacturers' marks command much more, especially if the illustrations are by well-known artists.

Designs by famous artists are popular with collectors, like this Louis Wain card depicting his humorous cat designs as Father Christmas.

TIP
Christmas cards depicting the humorous portrayal of cat images
by the famous artist Louis Wain are desirable, as are those by
Kate Greenaway.

Twentieth Century Card Collecting

By the turn of the century, cards started to depict imagery that fitted in with the lifestyle of this period. Many showed illustrations of motorcars, zeppelins and aircraft. Some collectors prefer to source just these particular designs especially as it crosses over into another of the major collecting categories – travel memorabilia.

FACT
In 1903 Professor Hubert Herkimer printed a car travelling at full
speed. Today this card is on show in the Victoria and Albert
Museum.

First World War Cards

FACT
During WW1 the sending of Christmas cards was banned at first
for security reasons and to ensure that paper was conserved to
help with the war effort.

Although the banning of sending Christmas cards was initially in place, the Government decided that this did not help the morale of their troops so they overturned this decision and ensured that publishers could obtain paper on ration. The other types of cards found around this time are those made by the soldiers themselves in the trenches and these are often referred to as silk cards. Aside from the obvious patriotic themes adopted there are many cards created for their sweethearts back home and these examples are very popular with collectors today. They would make them from ribbons and silks and embroider special messages on the front. Collectability is even more viable if a particular card can be traced back to the solider that actually created and sent it.

Patriotic themes were popular with WW1 soldiers who would design them whilst away fighting and send them to friends and family back home.

THE 1920S

This decade saw the deterioration in high quality elaborate designs with fine artwork due to the introduction of mass production. However, cards from this decade are still popular with collectors and some are single-sided cards (like postcards) with simplistic designs and messages. The 1920s also saw the introduction of lined envelopes. The idea was that these decorative envelopes would enhance the card itself but, as is common practice today, many

Dating to 1916 these silk cards are beautifully embroidered and were made by soldiers to send home to their sweethearts.

A embossed card featuring a little girl grabbing at the Christmas tree, it dates to 1924.

people just ripped the envelope apart to get to the card – thus lined decorative envelopes from this period are very rare.

THE 1930S

Although at the beginning of this decade flat single-sided cards were still being used they did phase out and folded cards became fashionable again. Generally made of paper or parchment some were also available created from heavier card much like today's modern examples. Imagery again was simplistic and varied from children, to seasonal scenes, and even humorous. Some of the envelopes bore printed designs inside.

POST-WAR CARDS

These patriotic themed cards were not popular once the war had come to an end as people wanted to put these hard times behind them. Fashion changed dramatically and people started to buy those that featured

A fun Dutch Christmas card featuring wooden doll people chasing a Christmas pudding on cutlery legs; bearing the slogan 'Race for Life'.

reproduction famous art or the still popular festive scenes. Quality was much improved and the card market began to flourish once again.

HALLMARK CARDS

One of the largest of the greeting cards companies is that of Hallmark Cards. Founded by Joyce C Hall, this young American began his career in printing by setting up a mail order postcard company around 1910. An instant success, his brother Rollie Hall soon joined him and together they set up the company Hall Brothers. However, it became apparent to Joyce that the postcard industry was limited as most people of the time wanted to write long letters rather than small notes which would fit on the back of a postcard. So the two brothers decided to add greeting cards to their line of products in 1912.

By 1914 they had purchased a small press and started to print their own Christmas cards rather than relying on the now poor quality European imports. Sadly a fire in 1915 destroyed most of their work and so the two brothers started to rebuild their business once again. Their other brother William joined the company in 1921 and by 1922 Hall Brothers was back to a thriving success employing over 100 staff.

FACT
Hall Brothers was the first company to advertise nationally as in 1928 they took out an advert in *Ladies Home Journal.*

During World War Two Hall Brothers' famous line 'When you care enough to send the Best' was born and in 1949 their company logo of a five-pointed crown was copyrighted.

By the early 1950s they were able to open the first of thousands of retail shops and in 1954 changed their name to Hallmark Cards Inc. even though the brand name of Hallmark had been used for some thirty-one years previously. In 1966 Joyce retired as CEO from the company and passed it onto his son, Donald Hall. Joyce stayed actively involved with the company right up until his death in 1982.

Today, we instantly recognise the name of Hallmark Cards and as you can image there have been billions of them made since the company began, including everything from birthday to anniversary and Valentine's to of course Christmas cards. So when it comes to collecting Hallmark cards what are the rarest, and which ones should we be saving now?

RARE CARDS

Hallmark have designed many special presidential cards over the years which are specifically for the President of the United States and his first lady to send out and so these are of course amongst some of the rarest cards you will find.

1963 JFK Card

In 1963 J F Kennedy and his wife Jacqueline only actually signed around thirty of the 750 cards supplied by Hallmark before that fateful trip to Dallas. When JFK was assassinated on 22 November 1963 the cards were destroyed by his secretary, Evelyn Lincoln. Very few dual-signed cards are known to exist but one did sell in 2006 for $45,000 thus making this Hallmark card probably one of the rarest in existence.

Winston Churchill Hallmark Cards

Hallmark approached the British Prime Minister, Winston Churchill, to see if he would allow some of his watercolour paintings to be featured on cards. Churchill instantly agreed

There is just so much choice with modern cards that picking which ones you like is purely down to personal taste.

and is quoted as saying 'Hallmark – A good firm'. These cards are now difficult to find and are the ones that collectors seek.

COLLECTING MODERN CHRISTMAS CARDS

There is no real hard and fast rule to collecting modern cards, it is simply go with what you like. In 2007 Daisy Chain Press released a range of Watermark Publishing Ltd printed cards inspired by the art deco period. I fell in love with them straight away, especially the larger ones produced for Christmas, which lit up when you pressed a button on the card. Very colourful, featuring stylish ladies in deco-style outfits with smart suited men, they are also printed with images inside. A huge hit when launched in the shops I strongly believe that this range will become highly sought after in the future.

In collecting terms, other cards to consider are those that already fit into other collecting categories, like the 'Me to You Bear' range or Disney-themed Christmas cards. Then there are those that are slightly more unusual with famous people on the front and the humorous ones that we all like to give. As I often say always buy what you love, and I think this is especially poignant when it comes to collecting Christmas cards. There are simply thousands available to buy so it is purely personal taste – if you love it then I can guarantee that there will be many other people that do too.

CHAPTER 9

FATHER CHRISTMAS

He was dressed all in fur from his head to his foot
And his clothes were all tarnished with ashes and soot;
A bundle of toys he had flung on his back
And he looked like a peddler just opening his sack.

Taken from the poem *The Night before Christmas* by Clement Clark Moore, c.1882

Father Christmas, dressed in a red suit trimmed with fur is a jolly, bearded man with a bit of a tummy. He lives in the North Pole with his band of elves who spend 364 days of the year making toys to give to all the good little boys and girls at Christmas. This task has to be completed by Father Christmas in one evening so in order that he gets to every house he rides in a magical sleigh pulled by eight flying reindeers, Dasher, Dancer, Prancer, Vixen, Comet, Cupid, Donner and Blitzen. On Christmas morning his job is done when all over the world children wake excitedly to find their stockings bulging with gifts, presents piled high under the tree and the glass of milk left for Santa empty.

The Luxberry Holiday Santa glass ornament by artist Mario Tarés for Christopher Radko®, chosen by Radko collectors as the top seller for 2008.

Fact
Rudolph the red nosed reindeer wasn't actually part of the original team that pulled Santa's sleigh. He was in fact created by Robert L May in 1939 as a character in a children's story. This story went on to become a huge hit and was turned into the famous song.

A larger than life festive character, Father Christmas has taken on many forms over the years from a gnome-like man to a beardless violinist. However, he has evolved into the character that is instantly recognisable as the jolly man in a red suit and his image adorns hundreds of different Christmas collectables.

THE ORIGINAL SANTA CLAUS – ST NICHOLAS

In the third century a boy by the name of Nicholas was born in the village of Patara (now the southern coast of Turkey) to a wealthy family. Raised as a devout Christian, Nicholas lost his parents to an epidemic at an early age, so as he grew older he started to obey the words of Jesus, 'sell what you own and give the money to the poor'. Having inherited a substantial amount of money Nicholas used this to help the poor, needy and the suffering. Dedicating his life to serve God, Nicholas was made Bishop of Myra and became well known for his generosity and love of children.

His reputation as a gift giver derives from a story about a poor man with three daughters. Back in those days it was the role of the father to find prospective husbands but as this particular man had no money, and thus no dowry to offer, his daughters were sadly destined to be sold into slavery. Very mysteriously, on three separate occasions a bag of gold (some say three gold balls) appeared in the home and would provide the much needed dowries. These bags had been thrown through an open window and are said to have landed in stockings or shoes which had been left by the fire to dry. It was of course St Nicholas who had saved this father's daughters and inadvertently started the tradition of children hanging their stockings around the fireplace ready to be filled with gifts.

Fact
Father Christmas is known by different names around the world.
United States – Santa Claus
Austria – Christkin
Italy – Babbo Natale and La Befana
Netherlands – Sinterklaas
Finland – Jouluvana
Spain – Papa Noel
Russia – Ded Moraz

Portugal – Pai Natal
Germany – Weihnachtsmann
United Kingdom – Father Christmas or Santa Claus

THOMAS NASH

A Thomas Nash illustration showing Father Christmas making toys in his workshop.

In 1822 the famous poem *Twas the Night before Christmas* (originally known as *A Visit from St Nicholas*) was written by Clement C Moore and described how Moore imagined Father Christmas would look. This poem then inspired the Elizabethan writer and illustrator Thomas Nash to illustrate images of Santa Claus which first appeared in *Harpers Weekly* on 3 January, 1863. This front-page illustration featured Santa visiting a Civil War camp. In the background of the image there is a sign which reads 'Welcome Santa Claus', and the illustration shows Santa giving out gifts to soldiers and children. Santa is sitting on a sleigh which is being pulled by reindeers and is drawn exactly how he is perceived today, with a long white beard, fur hat and a coat with a belt around the middle.

The most famous illustration of Santa by Thomas Nash was entitled 'Merry Old Santa Claus' which was again printed in *Harpers Weekly* on 1 January, 1881. This image shows Santa as a jolly old man, smoking a pipe and clutching handfuls of gifts. Nash continued to draw Santa Claus for thirty years and all of the illustrations created by Nash originally inspired by Moore's poem, helped popularise the image of Santa Claus, or Father Christmas, that we know and love today.

COCA-COLA SANTA

Another contributor to shaping this modern day image of Father Christmas was the drinks manufacturer Coca-Cola. In 1931 they ran the first advertisement featuring St Nick (Father Christmas or Santa Claus) in the *Saturday Evening Post*. The illustration was painted by artist Haddon Sundblom and showed this rosy-cheeked Santa Claus dressed in red. Many people believe that this Santa was illustrated wearing a red coat because this is the colour of Coke but in fact red was the colour interpreted by Nash's drawings. The idea behind the advert was to encourage people to drink Coke during the winter as well as the summer. So, the drinks manufacturer came up with the slogan 'thirst knows no season' and showed Santa Claus with the drink in his hands.

COLLECTABLE COCA-COLA CHRISTMAS

Pharmacist Dr John Stith was the brain behind Coca-Cola. On 8 May 1886 he produced syrup which he took to Jacob's Pharmacy for tasting. All agreed that this drink was 'excellent' and it went on sale for five cents a glass. Then carbonated water was added to give the syrup a more refreshing taste, which today over 120 years later, is still being enjoyed by millions of people right around the world.

As with any successful brand there also comes advertising and promotional merchandise. Over the years Coca-Cola and its bottlers have issued hundreds and thousands of colourful and fanciful pieces. Together these items form one of the most popular areas of collecting and within this vast range of promotional merchandise there are also a large amount of Christmas inspired pieces.

In 2006 Coca-Cola celebrated the seventy-fifth anniversary of the Coke Christmas Santa. During this year merchandise was released to commemorate the event. There are figural

Coca-Cola have produced many Christmas inspired promotional items including these festive beanie toys.

Santa ornaments, glass tree decorations and even a special edition collector's coke bottle with the Sundblom Santa picture on a red label. However, these anniversary pieces are just the tip of the iceberg when it comes to Christmas Coca-Cola memorabilia featuring the Santa image. Over the years there have also been trucks, postcards, beanie toys, glasses, crockery, snow globes, as well as tree and figural ornaments – in fact the list is endless. A great area of collecting that goes beyond the festive season there is something for every taste . . .

SOUGHT AFTER SANTAS

Coca-Cola is not the only manufacturer to turn this festive figure into a collectable icon; there are masses of Christmas collectables on the market devoted to the image of Santa Claus. Some are produced in figural form, whilst others appear as imagery on Christmas crockery. Then there are the many toys, decorations and even packaging all displaying this festive jolly figure.

CERAMIC FIGURAL CHRISTMAS SANTA

Over the years many porcelain and ceramic manufacturers have captured Father Christmas in figural form. Some stick to the modern imagery of the fur-trimmed red coat whilst others have used various colours and styles.

Royal Doulton produced their first Father Christmas figure in 1982. Entitled simply 'Santa Claus (HN2725)' it is the figurine that collectors desperately seek. The model shows Santa with his hand up a glove puppet and was designed by William Harper and stayed in production until 1993 when it was finally retired. Another piece depicting the traditional Santa is from the 'Classics' series. The Santa figurine (HN5040) shows Father Christmas complete with sack of toys and reading from a scroll, which is his list of deliveries; far easier to come by this particular model sells for around £80 to £100.

The Royal Doulton 'Bunnykins' collection has also included figural Father Christmas pieces with one of the more common being 'Christmas Surprise (DB14)'. This particular bunny is dressed as Santa bursting out from the top of a Christmas gift. There has also been a limited edition 'Father Christmas' bunnykins figure which was released for Christmas 2001. Dressed in a red Santa suit holding a gift,

The rare 'Santa Claus (HN2725)' by Royal Doulton, released in 1982 and taken out of production in 1993.

this piece was made in an edition size of 2,500 and is reasonably easy to come by, however, there has also been an unofficial rare colour way of this model where the bunny is dressed in a green coat which I have seen cost just over £200.

The Coalport pottery released a range of Father Christmas collectable tableau scenes and humorous figures inspired by Raymond Briggs' books *Father Christmas* and *Father Christmas goes on Holiday.* Four pieces were first issued in 2004 including the humorous tableau 'Where's the Chimney?' This model shows Father Christmas scratching his head as he tries to work out how to deliver presents to an igloo house which obviously doesn't have a chimney. This series was finally retired in 2005 with 'Christmas Begins' (which seems odd to finish at the beginning). This figurine of Father Christmas showed him with a bag full of letters under one arm and a sack full of gifts on his shoulder.

Many other ceramic and porcelain factories have also contributed with Santa inspired figures. Those produced by Lladro can be found in either the muted pastel colours or the more traditional Christmas red like the stunning 'Santa's Midnight Flight' produced in a limited edition size of 1,000. A real showpiece it shows Santa

The last figurine to be produced in the Coalport range of Raymond Briggs' Father Christmas was 'Christmas Begins'.

Lladro's 'Santa's Midnight Flight' is a beautiful showpiece that would look stunning as a Christmas display piece.

flying above the clouds as his three reindeer pull the sleigh. Some are produced by Nao; a line of figures released in 1968 under the Lladro umbrella. These too are very much in the Lladro style but are more affordable.

Wade is another manufacturer that ensures collectors get a healthy selection of

Wade produced just 100 sets of 'Santa and Rudolph' for the 2007 Christmas bonanza.

Christmas inspired ornaments with many produced in small limited edition sizes. 'Santa's Flight' and 'Rudolph the Reindeer' were both small issues with Rudolph only being available to buy through the internet. However, Wade joined the pair together in 2007 and produced 'Santa and Rudolph' which was made exclusively for the Christmas Bonanza and only 100 lucky collectors managed to acquire the pair of figures.

When it comes to fun, humorous Christmas Santa figures from Wade I opt for the one that features that loveable 1920s television animated star, *Felix the Cat*. A very small edition of just seventy-five, 'Felix

Christmas Surprise' shows Felix jumping out of a sack which is spilling over with toys and gifts. This piece was specially commissioned by *Collect it!* magazine in 2006 and was exclusively available to the readers. The edition sold out within days and is now very difficult to find as most reside in personal collections.

Toy Santa

There are many collectors of nostalgia and old vintage toys who also hunt out the harder to find Christmas pieces. One of the most delightful that I have come across is the very rare Schuco clockwork figure of Father Christmas. Having a tin flock-covered face and white material beard, he wears a white fur-edged red felt coat and black felt trousers, finished off with a pointed hat. Made around the late 1920s early 1930s, he is a real find for any collector and although he went unsold at the Vectis sale in 2005 I am sure if he came up for auction again he would make around £600 to £800.

In fact there are many old vintage toys to watch out for as nearly every manufacturer has produced something featuring Father Christmas. A very scarce piece is the 'Father Christmas and Sleigh' scene produced by toy makers Salco, although another manufacturer Moorestone also produced this design (which is believed to be earlier), dating to the 1930s. Other offerings have been produced by Trophy Miniatures. Their modern series 'The Christmas Specials' has a Santa Claus figure with a sack full of toys and a Christmas tree.

At the turn of the Twentieth Century marionettes (puppets) were popular playthings for children and the earliest example I have seen in the form of Father Christmas dates to around 1900. Made of wood his red and white costume was modern but this doesn't detract from the piece as it is still a rare and lovely item to own. He sold for £160 and is the perfect antique example of a toy St Nicholas or Father Christmas.

A rare and desirable Father Christmas clockwork toy figure produced by Schuco wearing traditional Santa costume.

A collection of vintage Christmas lead figurines including a Salco 'Father Christmas and Sleigh'.

An early 1900 marionette puppet made from wood and dressed in a modern-made felt Santa outfit.

Puppets remained a popular plaything with one of the most commercially known collectable manufacturers being Pelham. Founder Robert Pelham discovered he had a skill for carving toys whilst serving in the Second World War. Once the war was over he decided to set up his company and so from the late 1940s onwards he concentrated on making wooden marionette toys. One set that certainly fits into the Father Christmas category is the amazing 'Santa's Workshop' display sold by Vectis auctions in 2005. This single roomed house, buzzing with activity included a Father Christmas puppet with a plate of sandwiches and drink. All around him were other puppets including Mr MacBoozel in the corner with his bottle, two Dutch boys constructing a wooden train, Pinocchio nailing together a doll's house, and a clown with a large hessian sack full of presents. There was even the red nosed reindeer peering out of the stable door. The most amazing scene, it had obviously been carefully put together by somebody passionate about Pelham. A total one-off it sold for £800.

There have in fact been many vintage toys featuring Santa as well as a constant stream of modern examples. I can guarantee

A stunning Pelham puppet 'Santa's Workshop' display put together by a collector and then sold at Vectis Auctioneers for £800.

that when you visit a toy store near the Christmas period you will be bamboozled with an array of festive inspired choices. This is especially so when it comes to bears (see Chapter 15). Many bear makers such as Steiff and Merrythought dress these furry friends in Santa Claus outfits and have them featured with reindeers, bells and Christmas presents.

Collector's Tip

If you can't afford to buy the vintage Christmas toys then why not start a collection of old toy catalogues. Many illustrate Father Christmas on the front like the *Triang* Christmas catalogue dating to the mid-1960s. This is a more affordable yet fun way of collecting.

A modern Steiff Father Christmas bear in boot and a limited edition 2001 Steiff Father Christmas with Pony Sleigh.

Old vintage catalogues are a great thing to collect if you can't afford the vintage toys. This Tri-ang *Christmas brochure dates to the mid-1960s and shows Santa holding some of the toys of the time on the front.*

NOVELTY SANTA TEAPOTS

Christmas tableware is another section of collecting that sees the imagery of Father Christmas on many designs (see Chapter 9). There is however, aside from the huge range of gifts and tableware emblazoned with Santa motifs, a selection of novelty teapots carrying the image of Father Christmas. Teapot collecting is an area that gets both Christmas collectors and teapot enthusiasts excited because there are so many to choose from in the lead up to the Yuletide festivities. Some are of a standard unmarked variety whilst others are more highly regarded.

Carlton Ware has produced some of the finest with 'Flying Santa' being a favourite. An updated version of the famous 1970s 'Flying Red Baron' teapot this example has the Baron replaced with Father Christmas. There have also been other designs in novelty Carlton Ware teapots depicting Santa and one of my most favourite is of Father Christmas driving a car. They also have a range of golly Christmas teapots showing either the Florence Upton golly or

One of my most favourite Carlton Ware teapots is of Father Christmas driving a car.

a more modern looking golly wearing a Santa hat and being surrounded by gifts.

CHRISTMAS SANTA ENAMELS

If figural ornaments and teapots aren't your thing then there are many smaller items that may fit better into your Christmas display. Enamel trinket boxes look great as a collection and some of the most interesting festive ones feature Father Christmas. One of the most collected and established makers are Halcyon Days and since they began in the 1950s there have been many Santa enamels released. 'Santa over the Moon' and 'Teddies Christmas tree' were made as festive bonbonnières, which are three-dimensional figural confectionery boxes. There have also been enamelled traditional looking boxes some of which are musical like 'Santa Baby' and others illustrate more fun imagery like 'Elephant with Mistletoe' which shows the picture of a happy elephant dressed as Father Christmas. If a classic Christmas Santa is more your cup of tea then the 1984 annual 'Christmas Box' is perfect as it shows a picture of Santa in the middle of the lid surrounded by a border of holly and red Christmas stars.

Halcyon Days festive bonbonnière 'Teddies Christmas tree' forms part of their Christmas cheer series and shows a teddy bear dressed as Santa decorating a Christmas tree.

Trinket boxes are a perfect subject to collect as they are small so don't take up too much room and those made to the highest quality like Halcyon Days are always sought after on the collectors' market. When the design has been retired, these little Christmas gems are especially worth investing in.

Collector's Tip
Other enamel manufacturers of trinket boxes to look for are Crummles, Bilston, Staffordshire and Elliot Hall enamels. Try and buy those that are annual Christmas pieces or limited editions.

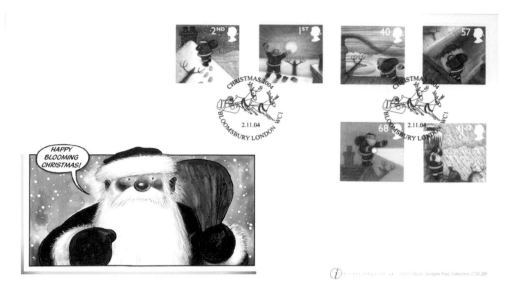

Buckingham Covers produce innovative autographed first-day covers with this being the 2004 Raymond Briggs signed Father Christmas cover.

STAMP SANTA

One of the most collectable of stamp companies is that of Buckingham Covers. Based in England they produce autographed stamp sheets and first-day covers purely for the collectors' market. A refreshing way of collecting stamps the collector is able to purchased limited edition covers that bear authentic signatures thus falling into the category of autograph collecting as well. In 2004 the author, Raymond Briggs, signed covers featuring his Father Christmas character. The first-day cover was entitled 'Happy Blooming Christmas' and postmarked at Bloomsbury (to go with the Blooming theme.)

SANTA ALL SEWN UP

Collecting Father Christmas memorabilia, as like most areas of Christmas collectables, is a mammoth subject area. Everywhere you look something will feature this iconic Christmas figure. Some pieces are by reputable manufacturers, others date from the Nineteenth Century, many are fun, and others are simple cheap unmarked ornaments that just look good on the mantelpiece. So as I continually stress it is really important to only buy what you love. Unless of course it's that five-foot-tall, all-singing, all-dancing Santa from the Christmas shop which won't even get through the front door – let alone last the season without someone removing the batteries.

CHAPTER 10

SNOWMAN CHRISTMAS COLLECTABLES

Another of my favourite festive figures is the snowman. Although here in Britain it hasn't snowed on Christmas Day for many years the tradition of building a snowman still very much ties in with the seasonal period. A character that is admired by children and loved by adults, the minute the first flurry of snow descends from the skies people rush outside to make their figures from the snow. I say figures because the snowman can also end up being a snowwoman or even a snowbaby – depending on what you use as facial features, a hat and around its neck. A symbol of winter and thus an association with Christmas means that snowman collectables are plentiful.

A Cherished Teddies 'Snowman so Deer' tableau figurine.

World Record

The largest snowman was built on 1 February 1999 in the USA. Named Angus, King of the Mountain, <u>he measured 113 feet and 7 inches tall and weighed 9,000,000 pounds.</u> However, the record was broken in 2008 when the largest snowwoman was constructed in the same state. She was named Olympia Snow and stood 122 feet in size.

A few years ago while doing research for an article I was writing I had the pleasure of meeting a collector who was fanatical about the snowman. This lady dedicated her life to amassing various items associated with this character and literally every room in her home was covered with snowman memorabilia – even the toilet seat had a furry snowman cover. Her fascination with snowmen was simply a memory from childhood that had escalated into a passion and was now the subject of her collecting hobby.

WALKING IN THE AIR

The most famous snowman and one of the most collected is the animated character created by English author Raymond Briggs. The Snowman originally began life as a children's book, which was first published in 1978, and was just one in a long line of books made famous by the children's illustrator and author. The animated twenty-six-minute long film was later released on the new British television station Channel 4 on Christmas Eve 1982 and caught the hearts of thousands of children around the world.

With no dialogue just genius animation not only did its signature tune *Walking in the Air* storm the music charts in 1985 when sung by Aled Jones but even up until present day this character has been one of the most popular collectables whose merchandise includes everything from ceramic figurines to pin badges and jigsaws to cuddly toys. This is why, quite possibly, The Snowman is one of the most sought after collectables of today forming one of the categories that falls into Christmas collectables.

This enamel The Snowman pin is just one of hundreds of collectables associated with this festive character.

ROYAL DOULTON SNOWMEN

The British pottery company Royal Doulton were the first to acquire a licence to reproduce this animated character into a range of sculptural based ceramic figurines. The first five pieces were released in 1985 which included one of the little boy James who actually built the character in the book and film (figure reference DS1) and another (DS2) of The Snowman on his own. Three more were released the following year and in 1987 a further five which started to make up the Snowman band. Figurines included the flautist and violinist with more members following in 1988. Another popular piece was that of the 'Highland Snowman' which was originally released in 1987. In 1988 he was mounted on a music box which played *Walking in the Air* – today this particular piece is worth in excess of £100. Royal Doulton then produced another five figures in 1990 making a total of twenty-three sculptural figurines for people to collect. The rarest Royal Doulton Snowman figure, which collectors are keen to secure, is that of the 'Skiing Snowman'. Released in 1990 this particular piece was withdrawn after just one year of production and so makes him one of the hardest to find. At one point collectors were willing to part with as much as £600 to £700 for this figure but today prices have settled down a little and he commands in the region of £300.

The other piece that collectors seek is that of the 'Lady Snowman', she was the second piece to be withdrawn from production in 1992 and again a few years ago she cost £400 but now commands between £100 and £200.

Aside from the actual figures, Royal Doulton also introduced tableware, including mugs, egg cups, and plates. They also added a child's hanging ceramic mobile and a series of plates. The rarest of all the plates is one entitled 'The Snowman Rides Again' which depicts the Snowman and James hurling through the air on a motorbike. If you manage to find on one of these rarer plates then you can pay up to £70, as opposed to £25 for the 'Walking in the Air' or 'Christmas Cake' decorative plates, which also form part of this range.

Amongst the rare items in the Royal Doulton Snowman range are a set of ginger jars which were produced in three different sizes and are very hard to find. However, the rarest piece that I know of is one that my partner Paul acquired. A few years ago he was collecting the Doulton Snowmen when he purchased a Highland figure on the internet auction site, eBay. When he received the piece he realised that this particular model of the 'Highland Snowman' was missing the red colouring

The Royal Doulton DS2 The Snowman™ figure produced under licence in 1985.

from his kilt. I was going to see the original modeller Shane Ridge at the Royal Doulton pottery so took this figure with me to have it authenticated. It turned out that this was a piece that had been missed in production and still passed as first quality not a factory second. Shane signed the base for me and said that we were very lucky to own what collectors would refer to as an 'oddity'. My partner had paid £180 and when a few years later he came to sell this Snowman he included all the information that the Doulton modeller had given us. This piece ended up selling on the internet auction site for a staggering £850. So it just goes to prove that collectors love anything that is a little different, especially if you have the provenance and know the history of the piece and it has been authenticated. So I think this particular 'Highland Snowman' figure is the rarest piece you will ever find from the range and is proudly on show in some lucky collector's snowman collection.

LIST OF ROYAL DOULTON SNOWMAN FIGURINES RELEASES

DS1	James	1985
DS2	The Snowman	1985
DS3	Stylish Snowman	1985
DS4	Thank You Snowman	1985
DS5	Snowman Magic Music Box	1985
DS6	Cowboy Snowman	1986
DS7	Highland Snowman	1986
DS8	Lady Snowman	1986
DS9	Bass Drummer Snowman	1987
DS10	Flautist Snowman	1987
DS11	Violinist Snowman	1987
DS12	Pianist Snowman	1987
DS13	The Snowman's Piano	1987
DS14	Cymbal Player Snowman	1988
DS15	Drummer Snowman	1988
DS16	Trumpet Player Snowman	1988
DS17	Cellist Snowman	1988
DS18	Highland Snowman Music Box	1988
DS19	Snowman Money Box	1990
DS20	Snowman Tobogganing	1990
DS21	The Skiing Snowman	1990
DS22	Snowballing Snowman	1990
DS23	Building the Snowman	1990

A SECOND COLLECTION OF DOULTON

Five years later, in 1999, Royal Doulton realised that 'The Snowman' character was still extremely popular, especially as prices had started to rise on the secondary collectors' market. They made the decision to release a further seven limited edition figures; the first being 'Dancing in the Snow' a tableau piece made in an edition size of 2,500 and featuring both the Snowman and James. A huge success, this limited edition was a sell-out and so others followed, including 'James and the Snowman', 'James Builds a Snowman' and 'The Adventure Begins'. The pottery also released a framed wall plaque and mounted in the centre was a ceramic three-dimensional model of the Snowman and James flying entitled 'Walking in the Air'.

It melted the hearts of many collectors when Royal Doulton issued their final ceramic figure 'The Journey Ends' in 2002 and it sold out almost immediately as collectors believed this to be the final figure available to them. Fortunately for collectors this was not the case or the end of the journey as a host of other collectable treasures became available on the market.

Royal Doulton Limited Editions

Dancing in the Snow
James and The Snowman
James Builds a Snowman
The Adventure Begins
Walking in the Air Plaque
Dressing the Snowman
The Journey Ends

COALPORT THE SNOWMAN FIGURES

Another British pottery Coalport acquired the licence to produce fine bone china The Snowman products in 2001. Right up until 2008 when they stopped making these licensed products Coalport issued both general release pieces and limited editions. Initially these Coalport Snowman pieces were very quickly snapped up by collectors; especially the first limited edition 'Christmas Friends', which has long since sold out and reached a staggering £600 and more on the secondary market. This was equal to the price achieved for the earlier Royal Doulton 'Skiing Snowman' when it was at its height. Due to

Coalport 'Dancing at the Party' Snowman and James Tableau.

this initial demand Coalport continued with their figures to much success and the first selection included tableaux such as 'Hold on Tight' featuring the Snowman and James on a motorbike and 'Walking in the Air'. All of these new limited edition pieces sold out before they had a chance to hit the retail market. Coalport, much like Royal Doulton, didn't just stop at the sculptural figurines but also produced glitter globes, tableware, and even a ceramic advent calendar. However, it always seems to be the sculptural figures that collectors crave and even today collectors are desperately trying to find those pieces which they missed out on first time round in order to complete their collection.

THE SNOWMAN PHENOMENON

It is not just the potteries that offer The Snowman inspired collectables as there have been many other gift and collectable manufacturers who have seen potential in this animated

Festive Family Frolics forms part of Christopher Radko's line of core glass decorations.

character. The Scottish-based company Border Fine Arts usually renowned for their resin animal and agricultural creations also produced a range of The Snowman studio enamels. Highly collectable today, these beautifully enamelled pieces included various hinged trinket boxes, spoons and even miniature teapots.

British manufacturer Crummles have been making hand-crafted enamel boxes since 1974 and they too issued some limited edition boxes commissioned through Royal Doulton (Doulton Direct) featuring The Snowman. There have also been many ornamented crystal glass pieces produced including those from Crystal Treasures by Country Artists. These were lead crystal blocks which had laser etched scenes taken straight from *The Snowman* animated film. There was also an exclusive called 'Over Brighton Pier', one of the most famous scenes from the film, in which James and the Snowman fly over the top. Limited to an edition size of 1,000 this piece retailed at £49.95.

The German teddy bear manufacturer Steiff also created two special mohair snowman pieces, the first of which was called 'Dancing with Teddy' and showed the snowman wearing his trademark hat and scarf whilst holding a fully joined miniature teddy bear. The other was entitled 'The Skiing Snowman' and obviously had the snowman skiing whilst wearing ski goggles. Both are now extremely sought after by collectors of both snowmen and teddy bears: they rarely turn up on the collectors' market.

A more recent addition to The Snowman range is from Hidden Treasures who produced collectable pewter hinged boxes. Each of these wonderful boxes depicts The Snowman partaking in different activities be it playing in the snow, giving James a hug, or holding a gift.

TOP TIP
Original production cells from the 1985 film *The Snowman* are highly collected, some selling for around £250 to £300 each so are worth trying to source.

SNOWMAN STAMPS

For Christmas 2006 Buckingham Covers used Raymond Briggs' character The Snowman as a feature for a limited edition stamp sheet and first-day cover. Each of the sheets had instant appeal as it was created from original artwork donated by the author and some of the limited edition covers bore his authentic signature, thus adding value for being an autograph as well as a stamp cover.

The Snowman had already appeared on a set of Christmas stamps in 2003. This particular set was issued by the Isle of Man post office along with a first-day cover sheet. Buckingham Covers also released an alternative cover at the same time in a limited edition size of 1,000 which again were signed by Raymond Briggs. Today, the Isle of Man version

Buckingham Covers Raymond Briggs signed Snowman First-day cover released in 2005 to help raise money for the charity Childline.

has a very low secondary market value whereas the alternative sheet from Buckingham covers has almost doubled in price.

Collecting Tip

The most common mistake with modern first-day cover collecting is to buy them from the Royal Mail. They may be cheap and cheerful but they are not a sound investment and don't tend to go up in value.

Top Tips for Cover Collecting

- Buy the signed covers with signatures relevant to the theme of the cover.
- Make sure the signature is genuine. Some companies sell pre-printed signatures, whilst Buckingham Covers' signatures are all authentic and original.
- Store them safely in folders so that they will not get damaged or dirty.
- Buy topical covers that commemorate a time in history or those associated with a blockbuster film, TV programme or children's character.
- Buy them because you love them – but choose carefully and your collection should increase in value.

JAPANESE SNOWMAN

It isn't just in the UK and America where this figure melts the hearts of collectors. In Japan collecting The Snowman is big business and there are large Sega arcade centres, where people can play the games and win a whole host of The Snowman products commissioned by Sega.

I have only touched on the mainstream collectables for this character but there is so much more available for collectors. You can choose between key rings and magnets, board games and soft toys. Then each year you will find a box of Christmas crackers, wrapping paper, Christmas cards and even hundreds of variations on decorations. To be honest there is so much available that it is impossible to cover it all but there is certainly something for every level of collector.

OTHER SNOWMAN COLLECTABLES

Although The Snowman is one of the most sought after of snowmen collectables there are still many pieces available which feature the general snowman image and these are usually more affluent from manufacturers during the Christmas period.

Christopher Radko produce hundreds of designs in core line glass Christmas decorations and of course this means there are many snowman pieces to choose from. 'Festive Family Frolics' shows a whole family of snowmen huddled together and is a beautiful colourful vibrant tree decoration.

The Flake Family was a popular set of six figures produced by Wade and today collectors are keen to acquire them for their collection.

Wade often produce snowman inspired Christmas pieces with the 'Flake Family' being amongst my favourite. This set of six figures included 'Mr Cold Flake', 'Mr Chill Flake', 'Mr Snow Flake' and 'Mr Christmas Flake'; in fact they were so popular that they were also made in a miniature set of Wade Whimsie figures as well.

From 1994 to 1996 the 'Snow Family' were released by Wade and were made up of the snowman, snowwoman and their snowchildren. There has also been the 'Snowball Fight' in 2002 and 'Christmas Cheer' in 2004, both of which were released in limited edition number of 2,005 and were available through C&S Collectables who commission special pieces from the Wade pottery.

C&S Collectables also produced a 'Frost 'e' Snowman' in 2001 for their special 'e Wade' collection which was only available to buy over the internet from their site. This piece was

The Wade 'Snowball Fight' was released in 2002 whilst 'Christmas Cheer' appeared two years later.

extremely limited to just 150 pieces and depicted a happy smiling snowman wearing a black top hat and blue woolly scarf.

Other potters have also cashed in on snowman popularity and aside from their The Snowman™ range also produced some traditional looking snowmen pieces. Royal Doulton issued a snowman character jug and Lladro issued a delightful tableau of a little girl trying to converse with a snowman. Entitled 'Talk to Me' it was issued in 2005 and sculpted by Virginia Gonzalez. The German manufacturer Goebel have over the years produced a range of humorous snowman figures which include 'Snowman's Holiday', 'Snowman jumping over an igloo', and the 'Snowman après skier' which features the snowman having fallen over when trying to take part in this sport.

Wade Christmas Cheer.

'Talk to Me' was produced in porcelain by Lladro in 2005 and is a delightful figure of a young girl trying to converse with a snowman.

Other snowman collectables include a Swarovski crystal snowman figure, and Bilston and Battersea enamels who produced the 'Snow Family' enamel Christmas boxes. Another collectable enamel box manufacturer is Halcyon Days. Founded in 1950 they have been granted the Royal Warrants as the first ever and only Suppliers of Objet d'Art. Specialising in antiques, enamels and porcelain they make highly collectable enamel boxes using traditional Eighteenth Century methods. Amongst their many Christmas inspired boxes is one entitled the 'Snowman and Teddy', a round enamel box which shows a shattered teddy bear slumped against the snow resting from the effort of building the huge snowman, and an unusual snowman bonbonnière called 'Nelson Snowman' which shows the snowman in the form of England's famous naval captain.

SNOW BABIES

Of course you can't have a daddy snowman and a mummy snowman and not expect to have a range of collectable snow babies and this particular area of Christmas collectables stands alone.

The earliest snow babies date to around the 1900s and originated from Germany. Usually in the form of children, some can be found as adults. Covered in a white grout (which resembles the old-fashioned artex which we used on our walls in the home) it gives the look of a snow suit although many of the older figures were unglazed porcelain. The figures produced were generally white but occasionally a pink or blue one can be found which are more desirable but a lot harder to come by.

FACT
Snow Babies grew in popularity in 1909 when Admiral Peary trekked to the North Pole. They were then again revived in the late 1920s when Richard E Byrd flew over the South Pole.

Halcyon Days produce many enamel trinket boxes some of which resemble snowmen such as the 'Nelson Snowman'.

Snow babies originated from Germany in the 1900s.

Snow babies are a popular Christmas collectable especially ones like these two cake decorations depicted on sledges and dating to the 1920s.

Modern snowbabies are eagerly collected with the most well-known manufacturer being Department 56.

These sweet little snow babies are often featured partaking in activities such as ice-skating or skiing and originally were used as cake decorations. Production of these babies stopped during World War One but resumed in the early 1920s when they began to be manufactured in Japan. However these later designs were not as well made or as finely detailed as the early German examples.

Today there are a few variations in snow baby models but one of the most well known manufacturers is the American company Department 56. Their hand painted porcelain snow babies come in many guises doing all sorts of activities and there are many ranges to choose from as they are not all geared towards Christmas but mainstream collecting in general. However, the Christmas selection is healthy, offering ornamental figurines as well as hanging tree decorations. Look out for the small production runs and limited editions as these are more likely to increase in value rather than the mass-produced general ranges.

MELTING MY HEART

I speak to collectors on a daily basis and each one tells me the different reasons for their passion for collecting. For some it is the fun of finding a bargain, for others because they enjoy the hunt of looking for the next piece to add to their collections but most (including me) explain how collecting started in their childhoods. Perhaps this is why snowman collecting is continually popular as it is associated with nostalgia and the magical places in which people can disappear from every day life for a while. Whatever the reason might be I know for sure that Raymond Brigg's *The Snowman* may well have melted away in front of our eyes back in 1982 when the film was first released but his memory most certainly still lives on in the form of an abundance of enchanting collectables.

CHAPTER 11

COLLECTABLE CHRISTMAS CROCKERY

I am sure each and every one of us can admit to owning at least one piece of crockery adorned with some sort of Christmas image. It might just be the Santa mug that Aunty Mabel bought you last year or alternatively a quality ceramic pudding dish which has an ornate holly and ivy design. I know for me it is a Royal Worcester reindeer mug, and an unnamed snack dish showing the image of a fairy making a snowman in each section, both of which spend eleven months of the year stuffed at the back of the kitchen cupboard. But like most people, come December I start drinking tea out of the mug and happily fill the dish with nuts, crisps and sweets.

When it comes to decorative Christmas crockery there is so much to choose from as every shape and design imaginable is available to buy. You can choose from teapots, mugs, plates, tureens, and even festive shaped decorative dishes. Some of the crockery is quite expensive as made by well-established factories like Spode or Portmerion, whilst other pieces at the cheaper end of the market cater for the more affordable pocket.

Everyone has at least one piece of festive crockery hiding at the back of their cupboards. Mine is this Royal Worcester 'Christmas Cheer' mug designed by Claire Mackie.

There are also a host of different designs to choose from. Some manufacturers tend to stick with more traditional classic Christmas scenes whilst others add humour to their designs. Then there are those pieces geared towards the younger generations as fun festive gifts, and other items are exclusively produced with the collector in mind.

ANNUAL CHRISTMAS PLATE

One of the hottest areas of Christmas collecting is of Annual Christmas plates. Cherished by generations, they first became commercially popular with collectors in the 1960s and 1970s. Today, there is still a very strong market for these festively decorative pieces and collectors wait eagerly each year to acquire the next plate to add to their ever-growing collections.

Fact
The rich Danish landowners used to gift Christmas food to the families who worked and lived on their property. After a while the food started to be delivered on decorative wooden painted plates, which the families would keep and sometimes display, much like modern collectors do today.

BING & GRONDAHL

In 1895 the Danish porcelain manufacturer Bing & Grondahl was not only the first company ever to issue an annual decorative Christmas plate but also the first manufacturer

The first ever Christmas Plate 'Behind the Frozen Window' dating to 1895 by the Danish porcelain manufacturer Bing & Grondahl.

to produce a limited edition. The story goes that one day the Director ordered his workers to destroy the mould for the small seven-inch blue and white glazed Christmas plate 'Behind the Frozen Window' which had been designed by F A Hallin. This act then ensured that supply was limited and in return demand was high. Today, this rare Christmas plate is still highly sought after and collectors are willing to pay in excess of £2,000 to own one.

Such was the success of the first Christmas plate for Bing & Grondahl that the following year 'New Moon over Snow Covered Trees' was released and then in 1897 'Christmas Meal of the Sparrows' appeared. Today these early plates are also highly regarded in collectors' circles and can achieve in the region of £800 to £1,000 each.

In 1908 Bing & Grondahl issued the first of their bigger twelve-inch Christmas plates, these also appeared in 1909, 1910 and 1911. However one of the rarest examples made by this company were the foreign 'Icelandic Christmas Plates'. Produced in 1928, 1929 and

The extremely rare 1930 'Icelandic Christmas Plate' made by Bing & Grondahl.

1930 it is not known how many were made or indeed how many still exist but if one does come up for sale it can make as much as $10,000 to $13,000.

In the latter part of the Twentieth Century Bing & Grondahl released many variations to their ranges of Christmas crockery and annual plates. In 1989 a range of 'Santa Claus' plates were released; this included 'Santa's Workshop', 'Santa's Sleigh', and the final one produced in this series, 'Christmas Stories' dating to 1994. In 1995 the series changed to 'Christmas around the World' and this collection ran until the year 2000.

Other Christmas plate series by Bing & Grondahl to look out for.

- Christmas Jubilee Plates; issued 1915, production ceased 2005 (the rarest being the 1940 'Three Wise Men' plate)
- 'Christmas in America' plates; issued 1986, production ceased 2003
- 'The Snow Fairies'; issued 2001, production ceased 2005
- 'Christmas Plaquettes'; issued 1999, ceased production after 2007 issue

RORSTRAND

The Swedish pottery Rorstrand was founded in 1726 and was the second porcelain factory to be established in Europe. Their first Christmas plate series began in 1904 and the well-known 'Blue Square' Christmas plate series started in 1968 and ended in 1999. In the year 2000, Rorstrand replaced their traditional Christmas plate with an annual series of the 'Ten Commandments'. Illustrated by Kerstin Holmstedt each is part of a collectable series; which ranges from the first commandment to the last, with passages from the Bible describing people then and now.

PORSGRUND

One pottery that cannot be ignored when discussing decorative Christmas plates is Porsgrund. Founded in 1885 by Johan Jeremiassen, this Norwegian pottery followed the example led by Bing & Grondahl and released their first Christmas plate in 1909, which was limited to just 250. However, for some reason they did not decide to release another annual Christmas plate until 1968. This particular plate, 'Church', was also produced in a limited edition and was to be the first in a long line of annual Christmas plates by Porsgrund, which are still released each and every year.

ROYAL COPENHAGEN

One of the most prestigious factories, that not only produce outstanding decorative Christmas plates but also an extensive collection of Christmas inspired pieces, is the Danish porcelain pottery, Royal Copenhagen.

Originally known as The Royal Danish Porcelain factory, Royal Copenhagen was founded in 1775, by the chemist Frantz Heinrich Muller. A specialist in mineralogy he had spent many years experimenting with hard feldspar porcelain made from kaolin, feldspar and quartz. Eventually he mastered the production of this coveted hard porcelain and approached potential investors. Initially very little interest was shown but Queen Dowager Juliane Marie and her son Frederik instantly recognised the potential of Frantz's company and so agreed to become partners.

During the first few years however, the pottery was beset with difficulties. Lack of experience, unsuccessful firings, poor raw materials and disappointing experiments were some of the damaging factors but eventually these were overcome when in 1779 the absolute monarch King Christian VII assumed financial responsibility. The pottery continued to be run by the Royal family until 1868 when it eventually passed into private hands.

ARNOLD KROG

In 1856 the architect and painter Arnold Krog was appointed as manager of the Royal Danish Company with his initial task being to take this porcelain manufacturer forward. Krog developed a new technique that allowed under-glaze painting and this new method made it possible to decorate the porcelain with various landscape and naturalistic scenes. The new under-glaze decoration was then shown at the 1889 World Exhibition with the knock-on effect of the pottery suddenly being projected into world fame.

Fact
In 1987 The Danish Porcelain factory merged with Bing & Grøndahl (established 1853) and became known as Royal Copenhagen.

A CHRISTMAS CENTENARY

The first Christmas plate from the Royal Copenhagen pottery 'Mary with Child' was designed by Christian Tomsen and released in 1908. This range is still going strong today, and 2008 marked the centenary of Royal Copenhagen's tradition of making Christmas plates. Still produced in the traditional method as 100 years ago, each plate starts with an artist drawing the motif. This then goes to the modelling shop where it is transferred free-hand to a plaster model. Once the model has been cut from the drawing, copies are made and then the plate itself is moulded. In order for the plate to obtain the blue glaze that Royal Copenhagen is so famed for, a special spray technique is used. Several thin coats are carefully applied and then partially brushed off again. This clever technique creates the different shades of blue which really shine through the plate when it has been covered in a clear top glaze.

The original 1908 Christmas plate produced by Royal Copenhagen entitled 'Mary with Child.'

Other Christmas plate series by Royal Copenhagen to look out for

- 'Christmas in Denmark'; first issued 1991, ceased production 1996
- 'Children's Christmas'; first issued 1998, to date
- 'Hearts of Christmas'; first issued 2006, to date

SPODE

Another ceramic company to celebrate its anniversary of the Christmas plate in 2008 was Spode. First issued in 1938, the 'Christmas Tree' motif has become more than just a design; it is a seventy-year-old tradition in Christmas tableware. Over this period it has appeared on hundreds of various giftware and tableware shapes ranging from cookie jars to teapots and mugs to Christmas tree shaped dishes. To commemorate this anniversary Spode released a collector's plate as part of their range. This plate featured the tree design in the middle but this time had a new annual border decorated in Christmas roses and mistletoe.

So popular is the 'Christmas Tree' pattern that it has also appeared in the 'Christmas Tree Disney' range produced by Spode, which sadly is now discontinued. The only slight difference to this particular collection is that the design features everyone's favourite Disney characters; Mickey Mouse, Minnie Mouse, Goofy, Pluto and Donald Duck singing Christmas carols around the famous Spode tree. However, if either of these ranges still

Spode has been producing its Christmas tree range on both giftware and tableware since 1938.

The Christmas tree range is so popular that it has appeared in many different forms. One being the Disney design where the characters were depicted singing carols around the tree.

hasn't got you in the Christmas spirit, then Spode have also run a range of 'Santa's of the World' which began with the British Santa in 1998 and finished in 2004 with the American Santa. As well as the 'Christmas Star' design which is unique star-shaped pieces with a pierced Christmas tree and the 'Christmas Tree Ribbon' which features a vibrant red ribbon pattern tied into bows as part of the border design.

Fact
Josiah Spode developed the formula for Fine Bone China which made the name Spode famous throughout the world.

ROYAL WORCESTER

Founded in 1751 by a group of fifteen men headed by Dr John Wall, Royal Worcester is another prestigious pottery that understands the need for Christmas inspired crockery. Over the years they have produced many different designs but one of the most popular in collecting circles is the 'Christmas Tales' series, which started in 1994. This range included plates, mugs, candles and even hinged boxes. Another of my favourite ranges from the Royal Worcester pottery is the humorous pieces designed by Clare Mackie. Raised on a farm in Scotland all of Claire's designs feature fanciful characters and are full of fun and sentiment. The design on the mug I own is called 'Festive Cheer' and features comical

Claire Mackie's Christmas inspired range of crockery for Royal Worcester is fun and humorous.

reindeers drinking wine with their antlers decorated in mistletoe, holly and even Christmas trees. There is also another mug 'Can-Can' which shows the same reindeers dancing the cancan with Father Christmas – I wonder if this is after they have drunk all the wine?

PORTMERION

The Portmerion pottery boasts many collectors of both its modern and older tableware ranges. Many choose to specialise in specific eras like the 1960s totem-shaped pieces, whilst others prefer the more classic 'Botanic Garden' pattern. Whatever your preference there is something to attract every collector's eye as Portmerion also offers a superb range in Christmas tableware to satisfy those passionate about this seasonal time of year.

Over the years the pottery Portmerion have issued many festive themed tableware including the 'Holly and Ivy' range which is inscribed with flowing script from the carol.

Acclaimed artist and ceramic designer Susan A Winget illustrated a range for the well known Portmerion pottery. 'Christmas Story' features a series of intricately detailed images inspired by the rhyme *'Twas The Night Before Christmas*. This treasured collection, which was originally only available to buy in America but is now available in the United Kingdom, continues to grow year on year with more pieces being added to the range. Recent new additions are a ceramic cake server, tea for one, and a mug and coaster set.

The 'Holly and the Ivy' taken from the Christmas carol is another of Portmerion's delightful festive inspired ranges. This pattern depicts antique illustrations and flowing script taken from the original Christmas carol, ensuring that you will never forget the true meaning of Christmas.

EMMA BRIDGEWATER

One of the best contemporary ceramicists of our time is Emma Bridgewater. Together with her husband, the designer Matthew Rice, they work from a pottery in Stoke-on-Trent making contemporary and innovative tableware. As a symbol of modern life there have been many different shapes and designs since the pottery was founded in 1985.

Christmas designs that are worth seeking out are 'Kitty's Christmas Pattern', 'Big Holly', and the 'Friends and Family' Christmas range featuring images of robins. You can also choose between variations in tableware design decorated in these patterns such as four-cup teapots, cow creamers, coffee mugs, and even Christmas pudding basins.

The oversized teapot in 'Big Holly' pattern is by contemporary potter Emma Bridgewater who has produced some wonderful seasonal tableware in various designs and shapes and patterns.

FACT

In 2007 Emma Bridgewater supplied some unique pieces for the Richard Dennis – A Potted History Sale at Bonhams in London. A huge success her work sold to avid collectors and Richard Dennis is quoted as saying that Bridgewater's designs are 'for every occasion – contemporary, commemorative and nostalgic.'

ASHTON POTTERY

Based in Oxfordshire, Ashton Pottery also has some attractive seasonal pottery on offer. Everything is made, designed and painted at Kingsway Farm, Ashton, England, in a restored stable block and barn. Traditional techniques are used and their festive selection of tableware shows images of Christmas trees and wonderful plump Christmas puddings.

SALLY TUFFIN – DENNIS CHINAWORKS

Renowned for creative thinking and producing high quality innovative designs, Dennis Chinaworks are a leading contemporary art pottery based in Somerset, England. Although not particularly known for producing Christmas inspired pieces the designer, Sally Tuffin, did create three stunning vases in 2002 that fit loosely into Christmas ceramics. Not strictly tableware but most definitely a collector's must-have these vases were illustrated with angels inspired by the work of William Morris, father of the arts and crafts period. Entitled

Ashton Pottery produce some fun festive designs on their tableware.

The three stunning angel vases inspired by William Morris and created by ceramic designer Sally Tuffin for her pottery Dennis Chinaworks.

Gabriel, Raphael and Uriel each vase measured 25cm high and retailed at just over £350 each. Today, Dennis Chinaworks are one of the most successful British art potteries in existence and their creations are prized items. So much so, that in 2007 a piece entitled 'Penguin Huddle' made a staggering hammer price of £17,500 at a Bonhams sale in London. This record price for a contemporary potter was an astonishing achievement for Sally and her team.

Other Manufacturers of Christmas Crockery and Annual Plates worth collecting

- Avon
- Beswick 1970s Christmas plates
- Hummel
- Jim Shore
- Norman Rockwell
- Rosenthal – including Versace Christmas charger plates and Bjorn Wimbland plates
- Royal Crown Derby
- Royal Doulton – including Brambly Hedge Christmas Plates and crockery
- Villeroy & Boch
- Wedgwood – including Beatrix Potter Christmas Plates and crockery

Many manufacturers have produced Christmas inspired crockery with some decorated with children's characters like this Wedgwood 'Peter Rabbit' Christmas plate.

FESTIVE TABLE

If you are looking for an alternative collection then Christmas plates are ideal as you can source modern ones to start off with and then invest time trying to locate the more hard to find antique and vintage examples. This collecting hobby would certainly keep you busy as there are so many beautiful annual Christmas plates around to choose from.

However, if Christmas plate collecting is not for you but you still would like some of the crockery mentioned what better way than purchasing a few pieces to use on the traditional Christmas Day dinner table. You can stick to one particular manufacturer for continuity, or if a little bit more ambitious you can use a cross section of different potteries designs: this is a fun way to decorate the table and imagine how surprised your guests will be when they find each has a different collectable plate from which to eat their turkey.

CHAPTER 12

CRACKERS ABOUT CHRISTMAS

No Christmas dinner table would be complete without one of the Great British traditions – Christmas crackers. Each year we all gather around and politely ask the person sitting next to us if they would pull a cracker. Then out floats the corny jokes, the even more tacky gifts and of course the unflattering coloured paper hats. These hats tend to then stay on our heads throughout the rest of the day and those that were either lucky enough or perhaps unfortunate enough to get the black plastic moustache apply it under the nose and try and make the others laugh. So where did this unusual tradition evolve from? Why does it only occur at Christmas and who came up with the idea of paper crackers which went bang when you pulled them apart? And of course more importantly are older boxes of crackers as well as modern, worth anything on the collectables market?

THE BONBONS

In the early 1830s a young boy by the name of Tom Smith began work as a baker and confectioner in London. His main interest was in cake decoration and in his spare time he would work on new ideas. Before too long he became successful in the art of cake decorations and so was able to set up his own business in Clerkenwell, London.

An adventurous young man he loved to travel and on a trip to Paris in the 1840s he discovered a sweet by the name of a bonbon, which in effect was a sugared almond. This sweet was wrapped in twists of coloured paper; a new idea which Tom thought could work well in the UK, as up until that point most sweets were sold loose and in paper bags. Bringing the sugared almonds back to England he began to sell them in his shop. The only slight problem was that these sweets sold extremely well over the Christmas period but sales virtually stopped once the festive season had finished.

Determined to make the sweets a success he came up with the innovative idea of placing a love motto within the paper and persuaded his regular clients to purchase them. This small addition ensured that his sales increased and he could afford to employ more staff.

However the sweets still sold much better during Christmas than at any other time of the

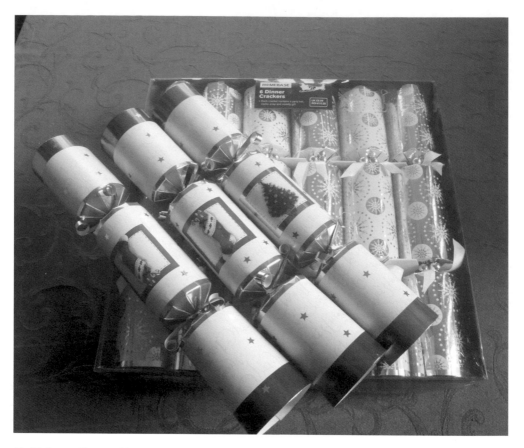

No Christmas dinner table would be complete without a box of festive crackers.

year so Tom set about trying to develop ideas to cash in on making more sales during the Christmas period. The flash of inspiration came one day when he threw a log onto his burning fire. A big crackle came from the log, which made Tom jump. This sound was the necessary spark that he had been looking for in order to make his bonbon more desirable to the buyers; but now he had to find out how he could create the bang that would add excitement to this sweet.

An Explosive Success

It took around two years for Tom to finally discover that if a strip of saltpetre, something familiar in today's crackers, was pasted to two pieces of thin card as each end was pulled the friction would create a spark and a crack. He had to do much experimenting though because sometimes they burst into flames, thus ensuring Tom had a few burnt fingers as he experimented. By 1860 Tom Smith had finally perfected his cracks and his 'Bangs of Expectation' were born.

Keeping the sweet and the motto inside but adding this noise gave his new confectionary a little more excitement which proved popular with the children and amusing for the adults. The buyers couldn't get enough of this new novelty sweet and he became inundated with orders. Tom then began to refine his concept. He kept the motto but no longer placed sweets inside the paper, instead he added surprise gifts. Tom then renamed his new innovative novelties as Cosaques because the noise made was similar to the sound of the Cossacks cracking whips as they rode through Paris during the French and Prussian wars.

The Cosaques, or as we know them today – crackers, were such a phenomenal success that Tom took the idea overseas. This wasn't such a good move as one Eastern manufacturer stole his idea, copied it and shipped a consignment of crackers to Britain just before Christmas. Tom was horrified but wouldn't be beaten so he set about designing eight different varieties of cracker. Working day and night with his staff they were ready in time for Christmas and were distributed right across the country. After this there was no looking back; Tom was now the biggest manufacturer of Christmas crackers.

Business continued to grow and it wasn't long before the company had to move from the original premises in Goswell Road, Clerkenwell to Finsbury Square, London. In the 1950s Tom Smith crackers was billing itself as 'the Worlds biggest cracker manufacturer'. Tom passed away in 1953 but his three sons Henry, Walter and Tom continued with the family business.

The three sons began to add their own development ideas to the cracker. Walter Smith, the youngest changed the mottos by introducing a topical note. Writers were commissioned to come up with topical references, which tied in with important events happening at the time. However, in time this changed from puzzles to cartoons and eventually the corny jokes that we now expect to find inside our Christmas crackers. It was also Walter who would spend hours sourcing unusual gifts and surprises to be hidden inside. One of his ideas was to introduce the paper hat. However, Walter wasn't the only one placing unique items inside the crackers, as the public also came up with ideas. In 1927 a gentleman wrote to the company, enclosing a diamond engagement ring and a ten-shilling note. He requested whether it would be possible to have the ring placed inside a special cracker for his soon to be fiancée. Unfortunately the man had failed to enclose his address and never again contacted Tom Smith. To this day the letter, diamond ring and ten-shilling note are in the company's safe waiting to be claimed.

FACT
Tom Smith was granted its first Royal Warrant in 1906 and even to this day has the honour of producing special crackers each year for the Royal Household. The designs and contents of which are a closely guarded secret.

GERMAN SILVESTERS

Around the same period that Tom Smith started to market his 'Bangs of Expectation' a German company by the name of Schauer started to make and sell their 'Silvesters'. Very similar to the crackers that we know today, they were longer and thinner. These crackers were made to place on the branches of Christmas trees rather than to be pulled and were very decorative as they were made from silks and satins. Although they did not have the bang element they did still sometimes contain gifts such as jewellery, handkerchiefs and bottles of perfume. People did continue to use smaller crackers to decorate their trees for a long time and I remember from childhood small crackers being placed around the Christmas tree branches.

CRACKING BUSINESS

Over the years Tom Smith became a victim of fire on three separate occasions, the first breaking out in the factory during the 1930s then again in 1941 when they were bombed during the Blitz. The third fire broke out in 1963 at the Salhouse Road factory – sadly these fires were a bit of an occupational hazard, and disasters waiting to happen, when dealing with highly combustible materials. Happily though it only took a year for Tom Smith to get

A box of 1992 Packateers Thunderbirds set of six Christmas crackers.

back to production after the last fire, and cracker production began again right up until the 1980s.

High borrowing became the downfall of the Tom Smith crackers and by the time the late 1990s arrived the company had to finally admit it couldn't carry on as a separate company entity.

One of the rival cracker manufacturers, Napier Industries, acquired Tom Smith in 1998 but they too suffered financial difficulties and went out of business in 2005. Today the International Greetings Group owns the Tom Smith brand name and the crackers continue to be made by one of the Greetings Group subsidiary companies Brite Sparks. Still popular with the public Tom Smith crackers continue to decorate people's Christmas tables much the same as they have done for over 150 years.

CRACKING COMPETITION

As with any successful business there are always others that want to get in on the act and Tom Smith had his fair share of rival cracker manufacturers over the years: one of the most famous being Hovells (some even credit the owner James Hovell of actually inventing the cracker although there is no solid evidence to prove this). The Caley Company was another rival, as were smaller competitors such as Mead & Field, Mason & Church, and also Neilson. However, at its peak the Tom Smith factory was producing 40 million crackers per year, dominating the market.

To prove how successful this business was just refer to the early catalogues. In one 1880 edition Tom Smith listed ninety specially designed ornate cracker sets, plus a further eighty which were plain rather than ornamented. The cheaper plain crackers containing only the sweet and motto retailed at 1/8d, around 8p today, whilst the more expensive variety was 42/- which is £2.10 in new money. These more elaborate boxes boasted elegant ringed crackers with wonderful picture scraps and contained well-made costume jewellery, which could be worn at the Christmas party. Even the boxes of these particular crackers were more innovative as they resembled a chest of drawers. Each draw was opened by a brass drop and the lid was decorated like the outside of a snowy window scene. The drawer was also clever because when it was opened a mechanical device rolled up to produce a festive scene from inside a window.

CRACKER COLLECTING

When it comes to the serious business of collecting Christmas crackers there are a few key things that collectors look for. The design on the cracker and the box imagery is important, also the novelties found inside define much of the collectability, and of course the obvious: that people only want boxed crackers that haven't been pulled. As with all collecting condition is important and the better the condition – not too much fading to the crackers or box, no tears and still with their surprises inside – the more money can be commanded.

Three boxes of junior Corgi crackers, which sold for £70 at Vectis Auctioneers. Includes '24 Adventures to Christmas,' and two other boxes of crackers with Corgi juniors inside.

FACT

All Christmas crackers are made by hand – even today.

EARLY CRACKERS

Early Victorian examples are hard to come by with most being in museums or private collections rather than readily available on the collectors' market. However occasionally you can find the surprise china baby dolls, which were a popular fill inside crackers at this time. A favourite Victorian saying was that who ever pulled the cracker that contained the china baby doll would become a parent themselves within the next twelve months.

There were also many themes to boxes of crackers during the Victorian period of the 1890s with Japonaiserie being quite prolific. These were inspired by the popular operas of the time such as *Madame Butterfly* and *The Mikado*. These cracker boxes were decorated with images of Japanese geisha and inside the surprises were miniature versions of Japanese pottery. These Japanese inspired crackers continued right through to the outbreak of the First World War and Tom Smith crackers often featured Japanese themes.

The themed cracker was especially popular from the 1880s until the 1920s with every design imaginable. Topical events were often used such as the 'Votes for Women' suffragettes. Two different boxed sets were produced – the 'anti' packs which made fun of the women and the 'pro' packs which joined allegiance with the women as they were made in the purple, green and white house colours of the suffragette movement. Even if a few boxes of these crackers survived they would be near impossible to find as both collectors of Christmas crackers and those that collect suffragette memorabilia would be eager to own them.

Other political trends featured heavily on crackers such as the ones made by Batger & Co. dating from 1885 to 1903, which showed the pro-colonial government minister Joseph Chamberlain – father of Neville Chamberlain – surrounded by flags and the slogan 'One Flag One Empire'.

Some might think it strange to have political characters on the front of a tradition that is in use on a day of peace and goodwill to all men. We know it would not even enter our heads to buy political crackers now – the last thing we want to discuss over Christmas dinner is politics – but when crackers first started to appear in the Victorian days this was the type of imagery that proved popular and made a statement about the times the people were living through.

It wasn't all political figures and events as many of the crackers were either extremely festive in design or, as the majority of Victorian crackers contained love mottos, many of the designs were also geared towards romance. The 'Bank of Love' crackers released by Tom Smith in 1884 was a popular choice with young people holding parties as the cracker box depicted a bank where you find love. So if the party hosts or guests were looking for a potential wife or husband these crackers were the perfect ice-breaker. The same design was also reissued as the 'Toy Bazaar' and 'Lowther Arcade'.

Other themes included 'Shakespearean' crackers that had contained quotations rather than mottos and hats from the Baird's plays, and even a box shaped like a trunk containing 'Mrs Brown's luggage'. There were also crackers specifically aimed at children like the 'Stereoscopic crackers' which housed tiny optical toys and kaleidoscopes inside.

EARLY TWENTIETH CENTURY – 1920s AND 1930s

With the turn of the century crackers became a little more sophisticated, with just one cracker hiding a winning ticket for a prize. Whoever found the ticket won the game encased in the cracker box lid. There was also a set of crackers which would have been popular with collectors today, called the 'Bric-a-Brac' cracker where a miniature 'objet de Vertue' was tucked inside each cracker.

The 1920s brought on a whole host of new ideas for cracker box imagery and the crackers themselves. On 22 November 1922 the archaeologist and Egyptologist, Howard Carter, discovered the tomb of Tutankhamun in the Valley of the Kings, Luxor, Egypt. On 16 February 1923 he opened the tomb and first saw the sarcophagus of the Egyptian king. This discovery fuelled the public's interest in Egyptology and Tutankhamun ephemera were available everywhere – including on boxes of crackers, which contained miniature mummy cases.

Crossword puzzles also became the 'in' mind game during the 1920s and true to form in 1925 a box of crackers containing crossword puzzles was released just in time for Christmas.

Another popular feature depicted figures of royalty. In the early 1930s a box entitled 'Our Charming Prince' by Tom Smith illustrated the future King, Edward VIII. The surprise contents also related to the prince as each crimson gelatine cracker contained either a small miniature bust of HRH, jockey cap, miniature stirrups, racing horses, motor cars and even cigarettes.

WAR TIME CRACKERS

During the Second World War restrictions were placed on the production of crackers. Tom Smith was asked by the Ministry of Defence to fold and tie bundles of the 'snaps' together with special string and official regulation knots. These bundles were then used for training the soldiers in armed combat as when the string was pulled on the bundles the sound replicated gun fire. However, just before production was phased out the distributors Cecil Coleman Ltd sent crackers out to our brave 'friends overseas' for a 'job well done'. These boxes were more of a propaganda exercise than anything else but the RAF to whom these crackers were sent each received an air force blue and silver bonbon (cracker) decorated with a sticker of a Spitfire aeroplane. Today, these are highly prized, and any serious Christmas cracker collector would give anything to own one, as they are incredibly rare.

POST-WAR CRACKERS

Things changed quite considerably for cracker design after the wars. No longer were there heavily illustrative elaborate designs or novelty inspired boxes like those of earlier crackers. Instead Christmas crackers were plain and simple until television started to take off in the 1950s and the main televised event was the coronation of Queen Elizabeth II on 2 June 1953. As you can imagine many boxes of crackers were adorned with the coronation and images of Queen Elizabeth, but this was something the Queen was already used to as even as a child she had appeared on crackers in the period between the two wars. One box in particular showed the young princess's face encircled by the garter ribbon.

Another company that started to make crackers during the 1950s was College Crackers. They began their business in a garage in Camden Town, London. Their main aim was to cash in on the cracker business where other manufacturers had suffered due to the blitz bombing. They weren't the only company to fill this gap either as a company by the name of Rainbow also saw the advantage in producing these utility crackers just after the war. Labelled as the 'utility' children's pillowcase fillers of the post war their humble beginnings grew until they both were making crackers on commission for much bigger companies.

However, it was during the later Twentieth Century in the 1980s that novelty themed crackers really took on another form and the elaborate yet sophisticated luxury crackers were introduced.

1961 Noddy Subsidiary Rights Co. Ltd paper scraps, which were for use on Christmas crackers. These have Van der Beek illustrations including all the characters from Noddy.

Higher quality gifts would be found inside these luxury crackers and they are often referred to as table decorative. Although they stayed the same in design, (plain and minimalist looking) year on year they can be dated by their colours as these colours usually go hand in hand with the particular interior colour popular at that time. So for example, electric blue and cerise pink were all the rage in the late 1980s and crackers were made in shades of blues and pinks; their surprise gifts were often of higher standing as well. One year Garrard & Co. Ltd filled their crackers with Mont Blanc pens and Crown Royal Derby trinket boxes. Of course these were luxury crackers, but still a nice thing to decorate the table with and they had the advantage of hiding gorgeous items: today forming two of the biggest collecting areas, pens and ceramics.

In fact there are collectors who concentrate on amassing only luxury crackers as they prefer to buy them for the items found inside rather than the actual cracker design. Prices vary from as little as £30 for a standard luxury cracker set, to hundreds for the more prestigious crackers with ultra luxury gifts.

One of the most famous names in luxury Christmas cracker retailing is the London store Harrods. Each year they sell many different ranges but always stock some high-end luxury crackers. Recently there were the 'Mary Antoinette' luxury crackers, which contained some sterling silver items like jewellery and cufflinks; these handcrafted crackers retailed at an astonishing £995 – which seems a little excessive for something that could possibly be bought just in order for them to go bang in about five minutes.

NOVELTY THEMED CRACKERS

The 1980s saw many companies take out licences to produce fancy themed crackers as the popularity of the novelty cracker increased. Unlike earlier ones which depicted political characters, romantic images and key events these were geared towards popular television programmes, especially children's television, like the older boxes of *Paddington Bear* and the box of *Postman Pat* crackers first released in 1989 and today classed by collectors as one of the classics. Other crackers to look out for are those of popular television programmes like *The Simpsons*, *Dennis the Menace*, *Dora the Explorer* and *Thomas the Tank Engine*. Each year variations of these are released and will definitely become sought after in the future.

Over the years there have been many different designs in novelty or themed crackers either focussing on a television programme, a well-known personality or even blockbuster films. *Star Wars Episode 1 – The Phantom Menace* film exploded onto the big screen in 1999 and of course a box of six crackers associated with this film was available to buy at Christmas.

Popular television and cartoon characters adorning crackers are a popular design with collectors.

Today this box sells for around £10 to £15 but is sure to be one that gradually increases in value if left unused.

Animation films are also sought after subjects with Christmas cracker collectors, boxes showing imagery of cult children's animated films like *Toy Story* and *Monsters Inc* are highly collectable as are those dedicated to favourite Disney characters. Each year the loveable honey eating bear *Winnie the Pooh* can be found decorating crackers and there are mixed Disney boxes depicting a host of Disney favourites. Aside from the actual boxes and crackers themselves there are also the hidden surprises to consider as many of these add to the collectability of crackers. For instance inside a Disney box will be licensed Disney products, which can only be found inside a box of crackers, so instantly people are buying the boxes for the special collectable surprises inside.

From the 1990s to the present you can pretty much find a cracker to suit any taste. There are those geared towards gardening and wildlife enthusiasts, some are based on board games, whilst others stick to the popular television and film screen offerings. There are also still available the more traditional designs and those with festive character themes like Father Christmas, scenes from the Nativity, and snowmen.

FACT
The world's largest cracker was made by the children at Ley Hill School and Ley Hill Pre-school in Buckinghamshire, England with the help of their parents. This massive cracker was 207 feet long and 12 feet in diameter. It contained a giant hat, a joke, 300 balloons and gifts for the children. It was pulled by forty-four children and the Saracens rugby team on 20 December 2001.

COLLECTABLE CRACKERS

Aside from all the themed and luxury crackers, manufacturers have tuned into the needs of collectors and today you can purchase special boxes of crackers deemed 'collectable' which are geared towards the collectors' market.

The British ceramics company Wade had a long-standing tradition of supplying the surprise gifts inside special boxes of Tom Smith crackers. These gifts were in the form of small miniature Whimsie figures, which Wade have been renowned for producing since the figures were first unveiled at the British Industries Fair in 1954.

The first set of Tom Smith/Wade crackers were released in 1973 and were entitled 'Animate Crackers'. This first issue contained a collection of eight Wade Whimsies that had previously been created for the Red Rose Tea promotion in Canada. Although the figures themselves were not new onto the market the actual cracker idea was and thus proved a massive success ensuring that more crackers were released in future years.

In 1976 the next set was released called 'Safari Park'. Again these crackers contained ten

A selection of Wade collectable boxes of crackers including Animates and Nursery Rhymes.

Wade whimsies, eight of which had been used in the past but two new ones, the musk ox and the lion, which have never before been issued.

By 1978 the 'Circus Animates' crackers appeared and these were unique as it was the first set that Wade had created exclusively for Tom Smith crackers. This also meant that Tom Smith held the rights of exclusivity for two years and no other company could use the specially commissioned animals which (apart from the seal) all stood on a drum base. After two years the rights were once again returned to Wade.

Then the 'British Wildlife' crackers were released in 1980, as were 'Farmyard Animals' in 1982. The models of farmyard animals used in the Tom Smith crackers were again made especially for the company by Wade, although the goose had been used previously in the Red Rose Tea promotions so Wade differentiated the goose by giving it a different coloured beak.

'Survival Animals' followed in 1984 and then in 1986 the 'Wildlife' series was released. A popular theme with collectors is that of 'Nursery Rhymes' which was issued in 1987. This set was issued in one colour glaze for Tom Smith crackers. The cracker company often took the spare Wade Whimsies that were leftover stock from ranges that had been discontinued or promotions that had finished. The figures were then re-coloured in the unique Tom Smith one colour glaze and the company would then place them in his other cracker ranges as extra gifts.

The Wade Tom Smith crackers continued to be a collectable success, and right through to the end of the 1990s there were various themes such as the 'Village of Broadlands' issued in 1988 containing miniature houses. 'Family Pets' was also a favourite in 1988 as was the 'World of Dog', which held two exclusively designed models of dogs for Tom Smith.

The 'Birdlife' series and the 'Snow Life' animals also appeared in the early 1990s and in 1994 'Tales from the Nursery'. Ten models were designed but as there were only eight crackers in a box two of the figures were harder to find ensuring that the collectablility went up as people desperately tried to find the two rare models. The same philosophy was applied to the 'Cat Collection' in 1996 and there are even rumours that different colour ways have been found in these particular boxes of

The Cat Collection of crackers by Wade joined Bear Ambition crackers in 1998.

Very sought after with collectors the Harmony Kingdom boxed sets included fairy folk as gifts. The rare Tinkibella is the hardest to find as only 200 were made in a 1,000 limited edition run of cracker boxes.

crackers. 'Bear Ambitions' joined the 'Cat Collection' and then in 1998 the 'Hedgerow Party Time' crackers and 'Sea Life Party Time' crackers were released. These were the last two sets of Tom Smith crackers to be brought out before the Tom Smith Company closed.

HARMONY KINGDOM CRACKERS

One of the most collectable modern Christmas cracker boxes you can find is that produced by British artist and modeller Adam Binder for the resin sculpture company Harmony Kingdom. Produced in a limited edition size of 1,000 these boxes were specially commissioned by www.thisiscollecting.com in 2001. Very much along the same lines as the later Wade Tom Smith crackers this box contained specially carved resin fairy folk which were concealed within each cracker.However Tinkibella. was very hard to find as only 200 of this mischievous little fairy were made. Thus everyone was buying boxes of the crackers hoping they would discover one of the rare Tinkibellas inside their box. The other fairy folk all had names Bellyfilla, Fortunetella, Crackersella, Donnastella, Stockingfella and the rather amusing Yurigella. I have seen the rare fairy make £50 alone, whereas a box of Harmony Kingdom crackers will only sell for between £25 and £125 depending on the season sold.

IN A CRACKER SHELL

Collecting Christmas crackers is an extremely enjoyable hobby as there is so much to choose from. There are those collectors who seek certain themes and others who source the hard to find examples. Some people prefer to look out for individual makers such as Tom Smith whilst many choose those that have interesting collectables actually hidden inside the crackers. Whatever your preference this is an area of collecting that is becoming more popular so perhaps when organising your Christmas table this year more thought will be given to the simple cracker and you might consider buying two boxes – one set to pull around the dinner table and the other to save for the future as certain modern crackers are sure to explode in price.

CHAPTER 13

COLLECTABLE
CHRISTMAS TOYS

Of course the magic of Christmas is seen through the eyes of children. An enchanting time of year when I remember bursting with excitement on Christmas morning waking up to find all my presents piled high under the tree. My brother and I were not allowed to rip into the wrapping paper until wc had sat down to breakfast as a family.

Vintage toys are keenly acquired by collectors with many making good money at auction, internet sites and collectors' fairs.

The anticipation and excitement was hard to contain but as soon as we were let loose it was well worth the wait as we discovered all sorts of toys, which would keep us occupied for the rest of Christmas Day.

Toy Timeline

As far back as the Ancient Greeks and Romans children have played with toys. Clay dolls and rattles, balls, hoops and spinning tops were the chosen play things. Many young people would play outdoor games using whatever was around such as pebbles, barrel hoops and even knucklebones but toy manufacturing has developed considerably since these humble beginnings.

The Eighteenth Century started to see mass production in toys and learning aids were a popular toy with the rich to buy for their children. These were usually in the form of puzzles, books and board games. The wealthier families also bought their children beautifully carved doll's houses and rocking horses that had real horsehair as manes. Toys that moved also became fashionable and the Victorians were fascinated with magic lanterns, kaleidoscopes and the thaumatrope (a disc with a picture on either side attached to a stick or string; when it was spun quickly the two pictures combined into one). The poorer children couldn't afford these new toys so would either make their own or save to buy skipping ropes, kites, or cheap wooden toys like spinning tops and peg dolls.

Parlour games were also popular during the Victorian era and those played were usually games of skill, memory, or wordplay. Blind man's buff was a popular fun parlour game; one person would be blindfolded and would try and capture the others who were desperately trying to stay out of the blind man's range but yet also teasing by getting close. Many of these games were also played during the Christmas period as after dinner entertainment.

FACT
Victorian parents would only allow their children to play with religious toys on Sunday.

Toy Manufacturers

It was also during the late 1800s and early 1900s that many of the large toy manufacturers were established like Britains Toys and Meccano/Hornby. Today these particular companies' products are highly collected with early examples commanding a premium, especially if still in original packaging.

Britains toys are renowned for their collectable sets of soldiers however they have also produced other items including Christmas figures like these early hollow cast robins.

BRITAINS TOYS

In the late Nineteenth Century there was strong competition on the market for mechanical toys. So a toy maker, William Britain and his sons came up with the idea of making toy soldiers. It was actually William Britain Junior, the eldest of the sons, who after much experimenting came up with a process of hollow casting these toy soldiers and in 1893 the first set of hollow cast was released. A revolutionary breakthrough in toy manufacturing this new process gave the Britain family the competitive edge they needed.

Today, Britain's is renowned in collecting circles; their sets of soldiers, farm animals and Disney characters are highly sought after, especially if found in really good condition and with original boxes. Although many collectors source these ranges, there has also been Christmas inspired pieces that are worth keeping a watchful eye out for such as the rare Nativity scene (Chapter 6). In 2004 Vectis auctioneers sold a boxed Britains Christmas novelty set, which included a hollow cast robin. Dating between 1932 and 1941 this set sold for £170, whilst in 2007 three freestanding robins (one had a leg missing) only sold for £25, proving that packaging and condition really does add value.

MECCANO/HORNBY

Any little boy would be delighted to discover a train set under the tree on Christmas morning, especially if it turned out to be an early Hornby model.

Liverpool born Frank Hornby obtained a British patent in 1901 for his 'Mechanics Made Easy' toy. The trade name 'Meccano' was adopted some years later for the playable construction system made from easy to assemble metal strips, nuts and bolts. Early sets of Meccano are today prized items especially if the No. 1 set, which I have been fortunate enough to sell through the auction house where I work. Obviously all the pieces have to

A no. 9 boxed Meccano set.

still be in the box and each box is clearly marked with the issue number.

Frank is also credited with making the first clockwork Hornby train set which consisted of a small Gauge 'O' 0-4-0 clockwork locomotive, numbered "2710", with a tender and an open wagon. Today these early boy's toys are keenly acquired by collectors with the price paid dependent on whether the train is in its original box, has all its accessories and is in good condition. The 'Hornby Dublo' introduced in 1938 is another set that collectors source. Originally only five boxed sets were available in a choice of clockwork or electric, with further rolling stock and accessories appearing the following year. Today collectors look for these early models and are prepared to pay a premium if found in original boxed mint condition.

LEGO

Most of us must at some point have received a box of Lego building bricks at Christmas. Originally invented by Ole Kirk Christiansen, the Danish toy-maker came up with the name 'Lego' (which is an abbreviation of 'leg godt', meaning 'Play Well') in 1934. Building bricks were not a new concept as children had played with wooden versions during the Nineteenth Century and rubber ones in the 1930s. However, this new type of building brick was made of plastic, had a tube and stud

The first Hornby train set was released was an 'O' Gauge 0-4-0 clockwork locomotive.

'Leg godt' is Danish for play well which is how Lego received its name and children will certainly play well and hard with the Christmas sets that are available to buy .

joining system and each piece of Lego can be played with another piece irrespective of when it was made.

Today, vintage sets of Lego sell well to collectors, those dating to the pre-1960s can make hundreds of pounds if in their original box with all the pieces present. Even modern sets are making good money, especially those that are themed like the 'Star Wars' and 'Harry Potter' Lego.

The Christmas sets are always well received both with recipients on Christmas morning and with the collectors' market. A boxed set of 'The Holiday Christmas Train (1073)' was released as a limited edition produced in the 9V series of trains. This model is decked out for the festive season in red, white and green with flashing lights and holly, it is even motorised and will move if you own the 9-volt equipment. Another range produced with a seasonal theme is the 'Advent Calendar'. Twenty-four days of holiday fun, you open a window in the specially designed advent box and also discover and assemble a figure or accessory on each of these days – with the grand finale being a huge model on the last day – Christmas Eve.

Five Fun Lego Facts

- It is estimated that there are fifty-two Lego bricks for every person in the world.
- If you built a column of about 40,000,000,000 Lego bricks, it would reach the moon
- There are 915 million ways to combine six Lego bricks
- Laid end to end, the number of Lego bricks sold yearly would reach more than five times round the world
- Approximately seven Lego sets are sold each second

THOSE HARD TO FIND MODERN CHRISTMAS TOYS

Toys have been a major part of children's life for centuries and today Christmas toys are an important part of the festive season. There are those that are specifically made for this particular time of year (like the Lego 'Advent Calendar') but there are also toys which become hard to find in the run up to Christmas. These must-have toys are usually those that nearly every child craves and so if there is not enough supply for the demand these items become near impossible to find.

TOY STORY MAYHEM

This was certainly the case for Christmas 1996 when toy stores became war zones. The iconic animated Disney film *Toy Story* was released in 1995 so the following year, 1996, the shops expected the main character 'Woody' to be the must-have toy for Christmas. Wrongly predicted it was actually the spaceman 'Buzz Light Year' that every child craved so all those parents who were unable to get their hands on a Buzz toy had to face bitterly disappointed children on Christmas morning.

The hard to acquire toy of the year in 1996 'Christmas Buzz Holiday Hero' caused mayhem in the shops with parents desperately trying to buy him.

Since 1996 Buzz has seen a festive makeover as he appeared in silver with a holly green trim as 'Christmas Buzz Holiday Hero'. He also spoke several Christmas phrases when you pushed his buttons such as, 'To the North Pole and Beyond', and 'This is Buzz Light Year, come in Rudolph!'

TOYING WITH TOYS

I know it's a really hard decision when surrounded with so many choices but buying toys, especially those connected with Christmas, is a wonderful way to start and build a collection. Obviously vintage toys are at the higher end of the market so it is advisable to start with more modern ones until you learn about your subject area. Also concentrate on one aspect of toy collecting. Look for what appeals to you, whether that be dolls, teddy bears or boy's toys; starting off in this way will help you learn quickly about that particular subject area.

Collector's Tip
Visit specialist toy fairs or auctions like Vectis. This will give you an idea of what is available on the market and the sort of prices to pay. This is the best way of learning because if you see an item in the flesh it will be forever embedded on your mind.

Modern Christmas toys are in abundance and will really instil that Christmas spirit. Some will bring back childhood memories whilst others will open up your mind to what is actually available. I also guarantee that if buying for children these festive toys will keep them occupied for the whole of Christmas Day allowing you to get on with cooking the Christmas dinner in peace.

CHAPTER 14

DESIRABLE DOLLS

One of the most popular girls' toys is a doll and these have been in existence since prehistoric times with some early examples having been found in Egyptian graves and tombs. The majority of early dolls were made of simple materials such as wood, clay, string and rags with papier mâché composition being used in the 1600s. However, over the centuries doll manufacturing started to become more sophisticated and by the 1800s doll making really came into its own with the introduction of wax and porcelain at the beginning of the Nineteenth Century

---

Fact
Wooden dolls otherwise known as 'peg-woodens' or 'Dutch dolls' were a cheaper alternative to the wax or bisque dolls and these were made right up until the 1920s.

It wasn't just the materials that evolved but the look of dolls also changed. Originally dolls resembled adults but in the 1850s the 'Bebe' doll was introduced and was the first doll to look like a young girl. The cost was also a problem as the French dolls were hugely popular but very expensive to buy so when the German bisque dolls became available on the market they were a welcome alternative.

Aside from the manufactured dolls, homemade rag dolls had also been popular with children and were usually made by mothers for their daughters. However, in the middle of the 1800s English and American companies started to make their own commercial versions of the rag doll.

Celluloid was used in doll making from the middle of the Nineteenth Century through to the 1950s. Hundreds of cheaply produced celluloid dolls were made in Europe, America and Japan. However this material was extremely flammable and easily went up in flames so was dangerous for children. The end of World War Two saw the introduction of hard plastic and although this was relatively safe it still had a tendency to melt if placed near heat.

Eventually vinyl was introduced and this changed the face of doll making. Hair could be rooted into the head rather than glued on and mass production came into effect.

DOLLS

Today doll manufacturing is big business and there are hundreds of different varieties and designs available to buy, both for children to play with and collectors to admire. There are also dolls made for special occasions and those released at significant times of the year such as the Christmas tree fairy doll, which I have already discussed.

However, aside from this tree topping decoration there are an abundance of different dolls released with a festive theme during the Christmas period. Each year manufacturers produce their regular line of dolls in a seasonal guise; maybe the doll is dressed in Christmas colours like green, red, silver and gold, or the outfits are trimmed with fur, glitter or tinsel. Dolls are also released resembling Christmas or pantomime characters meaning there is much on offer when it comes to Christmas dolls. Many of these are only produced during the yuletide festivities resulting in very limited numbers only being available over the Christmas period. This in turn results in the dolls becoming collectable very quickly, thus rising in value.

A Christmas porcelain doll wearing a festive white fur trimmed red outfit.

TEEN FESTIVE FASHION DOLLS

Of all the dolls on the market fashion dolls are definitely my favourite as not only do they bring back nostalgic memories of my own childhood but I also love the outfits in which they are dressed. I used to spend hours playing with my Sindy doll back in the 1970s and today the early examples of Sindy, dating from the 1960s onwards, and her original outfits are highly sought after by collectors.

Fact
Pedigree made the first Sindy doll in 1963. She was marked MADE
IN ENGLAND on or in the hairline at the back of her head.

One of my favourite fashion dolls, Sindy was produced in 1997 by Hasbro as 'Festive Sindy' dressed in a gold-flecked red gown with white fur trim.

Today this teen fashion doll is still going strong and there are often Christmas specials released. In 1997 Hasbro issued 'Festive Sindy'; she was dressed in a gold-flecked red gown with white fur trim and her hair was covered by a fur-edged hood. More recently, Vivid Imaginations produced a Christmas Sindy which was only available to buy through the retail outlet Argos. Again Sindy was dressed in a fur trimmed short red Santa-style minidress worn with a cap and cape.

Sindy's rival, Barbie is another of the popular collectable teen fashion dolls who has also featured in festive form. Two thousand and eight marked the twenty-year anniversary of the very first holiday themed Barbie doll. This doll was released in 1988 and she wore the most stunning red luxurious Christmas gown. An instant success with collectors the 'Happy Holidays' range continued with Barbie dressed in a beautiful

Two thousand and eight marked the twenty-year anniversary of the first holiday themed Barbie doll.

white gown with fur trim in 1989. The following year the first African-American doll was released in the 'Happy Holidays' range and she too looked dazzling in cerise pink. However in 1999 the range changed to become 'Holiday Treasures' and this year saw the first holiday themed doll to be available exclusively to members of the official Barbie collectors' club. By 2001 the Barbie to buy was 'The Nutcracker' which featured this glamorous fashion doll wearing a sparkling pink tutu and a line of nutcracker themed dolls were made available for everyone to buy. Created specifically for displaying rather than playing with these Barbie dolls have very quickly become sought after and so can command a premium on the collectors' market.

Interesting Barbie Facts

- Barbie's real name is Barbara Millicent Roberts as she was named after Mattel's daughter.
- The first Barbie doll was launched by Mattel Inc. on 9 March 1959 and she wore a black and white zebra print swimsuit.
- During that first launch year 350,000 Barbie dolls were sold.
- Barbie owns far more shoes than Imelda Marcos – there are over a million pairs.
- Two Barbie dolls are sold every second somewhere in the world.
- The 1965 version of the 'Midnight Blue' Barbie doll (actually dressed in red) sold for a staggering £9,000 at Christies auctioneers creating a world record for these dolls: the rare pink version wasn't far behind, it sold for £5,040.

PULLIP DOLLS

The highly desirable Pullip large-eyed teen dolls are made in Japan by Jun Planning. They too issued a Christmas doll in 2004. This beautiful wide-eyed doll was dressed in red with much white fur trim. She was also adorned with bells. Later a miniature

Made in Japan the Pullip large-eyed teen dolls are extremely collectable. In 2004 the Christmas doll was issued and was so popular that a miniature version was also released.

A special series of Cabbage Patch Doll 'Holiday Babies' were produced by Mattel which were dressed in various Christmas outfits.

version of this doll was released, complete with reindeer. Pullip dolls are extremely collectable with some selling for well over £100 although they are difficult to track down to buy in the United Kingdom.

CABBAGE PATCH CHRISTMAS

Many of the Cabbage Patch Kids dolls have featured in Christmas themes over the years. In the 1990s a special edition set of 'Holiday Babies' was released by Mattel showing the Cabbage Patch Kids dressed in various outfits. There was a red needle cord dress trimmed with lace, a white satin dress with net overlay sprinkled with gold stars, and another outfit of the doll dressed in green corduroy shorts and a red tartan waistcoat.

AMERICAN DOLLS

In America there are many companies who produce special Christmas dolls. Madame Alexander is a highly regarded doll manufacturer and in 2001 the company created two wonderful dolls to capture the Christmas market. 'Holiday Ballerina' was an eight-inch doll dressed in a ballerina costume, whilst 'Holiday Snowflake Skater' wore a red flock nylon dress with a full skirt decorated with tiny crystals in snowflake patterns. More recently, for Christmas 2008 Madame Alexander released the 'Holiday Magic Ballerina'; available with various hair colours each doll was dressed in a Christmas red tutu with matching satin ballet shoes and was available in a limited edition of 550 and retailed at $79.95.

GENERAL CHRISTMAS DOLLS

Many different manufacturers produce themed dolls during the festive period such as Woolworths who released 'Christmas Holly' sold under the Chad Valley label. This sweet baby doll was dressed in red and wore a Santa hat and crotched red shoes. There

Each year manufacturers release a variety of themed Christmas dolls so it is worth checking out the toy shops to see what there is available.

are also plenty of offerings from modern porcelain manufacturers and the soft doll companies but you need to visit all your local toyshops in order to see which ones appeal to you.

CHAPTER 15

Christmas Teddy Bears and Their Furry Friends

Don't forget a bear is for life and not just for Christmas!

Dolls don't always appeal to every child (especially not the boys) but one toy that seems to capture the hearts of children all over the world is that of the loveable, cuddly teddy bear and his furry friends. I own a small 'hug' (collection of bears) which I gain great enjoyment from and each brings back lovely memories of when I bought them. Bears have individual personalities and many collectors say that they only buy those that 'speak to them'. I can identify with this totally as there are so many to choose from, and in such different styles that it is important to buy those that you love and feel drawn to.

Bear Beginnings

In 1902 Richard Steiff, nephew of soft toy manufacturer Margaret Steiff, created the first jointed teddy bear. Before his discovery soft toy bears had been based on real wild bears from folklore stories. These were quite ferocious with bared teeth and children were scared of them so Richard's newly designed bear was a welcome sight because it captured children's hearts rather than frightening them to bits.

Using string joints Richard was able to produce a moveable jointed bear and after much sketching and experimenting he came up with 'PB55' – the first ever teddy bear. The P stood for the material used 'plush', the B was for *Beweglich*, a German word for moveable and the '55' was the height in centimetres when the bear was seated.

Richard's aunt was not convinced by this new toy and Richard was still not entirely satisfied with the design so he continued experimenting. Finally in 1905 Richard had produced a bear that he and his aunt were happy with and placed it into production. It was an instant

Richard Steiff originally invented the teddy bear that we know and love today in 1902. Today bears feature in many festive guises and are one of the most collectable toys on the market.

success with the public and by 1906 a staggering 400,000 of Richard's bears had been sold.

Richard's bear was referred to as 'Barle' by his aunt, Margaret, which simply is a term of endearment. The official name, as we know it today, of 'Teddy Bear' was in fact adopted after the American President Theodore Roosevelt refused to shoot a captive bear whilst on business. The story made newspaper headlines and a cartoon strip was drawn by Clifford K Berryman. Within days people started to associate the president with bears and had given him the nickname of 'teddy'. The new jointed bears had already begun to appear in shop windows and so Roosevelt was instantly associated with these soft toy bears and the public began to refer to them as the 'teddy bear', a name which stuck and is still being used today.

CHRISTMAS BEARS

Since 1902 the teddy bear has been the staple toy in every child's play box and just like dolls teddy bear manufacturers also produce their regular lines in various festive guises during the Christmas period. A vast area so I have chosen those bears in Christmas dress that I personally love the best.

HARRODS ANNUAL CHRISTMAS BEAR

Each year without fail I make sure that I take a trip to London in order to purchase the annual Harrods Christmas bear. Originally launched in 1986 these bears are now extremely sought after by collectors. Prices for the earlier bears vary depending on the year but the original 1986 bear can command as much as £600 on the collectors' market. In 2008 Oscar was the annual Christmas bear. Dressed in a cherry red Christmas jumper decorated with a wintry scene he is not only gorgeous but a definite investment for the

I am an avid collector of the annual Harrods Christmas bears which was originally launched in 1986. This 2008 plush bear was Oscar who was dressed in a cherry red Christmas jumper.

future, as these bears can only be bought directly from Harrods around the festive season, unless you are prepared to pay a little more for them on internet auction sites and collectors' fairs.

Aside from the affordable plush variety (under £25) there is normally an exact replica of the Harrods Christmas bear made by the prestigious German bear manufacturer Steiff. Available as a limited edition it is identical to the plush variety but is made of mohair, has the Steiff button in the ear and is available in a small limited edition size. This bear is more expensive (just under £100) but is far superior to the more affordable plush variety and both teddy bear collectors and those of Christmas memorabilia clamber to own these special bears.

Steiff produce exclusive bears for Harrods all year round but it is the Christmas ones that appeal to me most, especially the more recently released 'Father Christmas in a Chimney' which shows a lovely gold-blonde mohair bear dressed in a Santa suit, wriggling down a chimney with his Christmas sack full of presents.

STEIFF

In general, Steiff produce some of the most exquisite bears on the market and some of the most unusual. One Christmas bear, which I have to mention, is the 'Nutcracker' limited edition. The wow factor in this particular mohair bear was that it could actually crack nuts! Modelled on the Erz mountain nutcrackers, it possesses a screw action nutcracker inside its chest. To use you simply place a nut inside the cracker, turn the teddy's head and the nut is cracked. Retailing at a staggering £300 this is not a cheap bear to buy but certainly

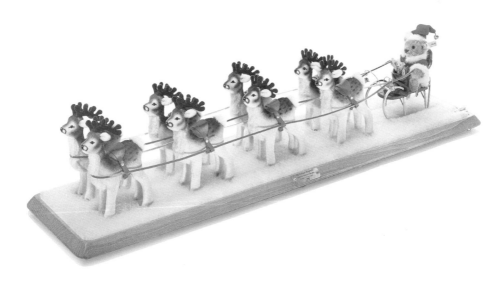

The Steiff 'Christmas Express' was limited to 750 pieces when released in 2006.

one for the history books for innovation, ensuring that it will be a hot Christmas collectable in the future.

Christmas 2006 saw the release of the limited edition Steiff 'Christmas Express'. Made in an edition size of 750 it features eight Steiff reindeer made of the finest cotton velvet pulling a sleigh. They have elaborately crafted antlers and red leather harnesses. The Father Christmas teddy bear sits in the sleigh wearing a coat and hat made from red velvet with a soft white alpaca lining. He is also carrying a linen bag filled to the brim with presents including the sweetest little teddy bear made of tin. This spectacular piece sits on a wooden plinth made from beech wood and is covered in the finest white mohair to give the effect of snow. A truly stunning Christmas decoration as well as a wonderful Christmas collectable this piece really is the ultimate for any teddy bear enthusiast.

FACT

The most expensive modern limited edition bear ever produced was by Steiff in 2005 to mark their 125th anniversary. Entitled '125 Karat' this prestigious bear has two cabochon sapphire eyes which are each surrounded by twenty Russian cut diamonds set in 24-carat gold. The fur is made from mohair that has been combined with raw silk and gold threads to give a golden shine. His nose and mouth are cast in 24-carat gold and so is the button in his ear and the medallion around his neck. He also came with a booklet, Mont Blanc pen and bottle of gold ink: all this for the staggering price of $25,000.

If you don't have room for a large bear tableau or would just rather own one of the individual Steiff Christmas bears then there have been many to choose from. Some are musical such as the 2006 Santa bear who is wearing a green velvet coat with gold waist cord and plays 'We wish you a merry Christmas'. Others are available in Christmas characters such as angels, drummer boys and even a bear on snowshoes, but the ones that I love best and think are great for collecting are the miniature Steiff hanging tree decorations. Still made in the highest quality mohair these tree decorations come in all different forms like the gorgeous 'Mistletoe bear' and amusing 'Snowball bear'.

MERRYTHOUGHT BEARS

When it comes to teddy bears and soft toy manufacturing, Merrythought is another major player. Now in its third family generation of owners, the history behind the establishment of Merrythought began in 1919 when WG Holes and GH Laxton opened a small spinning mill in Yorkshire so that they could weave imported raw mohair. The business was such a success that by the 1920s they were able to expand by purchasing Dyson Hall and Co. Ltd another mohair plush weaving factory located in Huddersfield.

In 1930 the decision was made to set up a soft toy-making factory as an outlet for all the plush material and this was when the company we know and love today, Merrythought Limited, was founded. A sales manager was employed and former Chad Valley manager, CJ Rendle was hired to look after production, and at this point only twenty factory workers were employed out of Merrythought's temporary premises.

However, in 1931 more secure premises were leased on the River Severn in Ironbridge and by 1932 the company had expanded to employ 200 people resulting in Merrythought becoming the largest soft-toy factory in Britain by 1935.

FACT
Teddy Bears produced in the 1930s were marked with a celluloid button in the ear.

During the Second World War the factory was taken over by the Ministry of Aircraft and British Admiralty to make maps and store plywood, so the toy production was transferred to temporary premises once again. By 1946 Merrythought was able to move back to Ironbridge and in 1956 they were able to buy the premises for themselves.

Still very much operational in this beautiful village, the Merrythought factory is the only commercial teddy bear maker currently producing in Britain. There is an array of different styles and designs available to collect from vintage to modern and the more traditional looking bear through to their infamous 'Cheeky' bears.

FACT
Merrythought's first teddy bear catalogue was produced in 1931 and featured designs by Florence Atwood.

THE CHEEKY CHRISTMAS

Of all the Merrythought range of bears, 'Cheeky' is my favourite. Designed by Jean Barber he was first launched at the British Toy Fair in 1956. This new and exciting 'Cheeky' was very different to any other bear that had been on the market before. A big round head, velvet muzzle and bells in his ears, 'Cheeky' automatically had a distinctive style, which is still instantly recognisable today. Initially he was issued in four different sizes and was made either of art silk, gold plush or mohair. Today collectors eagerly source the early 1950s and 1960s 'Cheeky' bears but there is also a strong market for the modern 'Cheeky'.

Over the years there has been an assortment of different 'Cheekys', some have had their mouths open, others are clothed and many have been musical like the 'Merry Christmas Cheeky Punkie' which was released as a limited edition of just 75 in 2007. Created in Christmassy berry red plush with a snowy white stomach and a brandy cream coloured

'Merry Christmas Cheeky Punkie' was issued with a Christmas card signed by Oliver Holmes.

British bear manufacturer Merrythought has produced many Christmas inspired teddies as well as innovative Cheeky Bear hanging tree ornaments.

topknot, he played 'So this is Christmas' when you wound a key. When purchased this bear also came with a Christmas card depicting the image of this adorable 'Cheeky Punkie' and had been signed by Merrythought's current owner Oliver Holmes.

The Merrythought factory is also well known with collectors for their traditional bears, and for Christmas 2008 a snowy white version was released. This bear had the footmark 'Merry Christmas 2008' in Christmas colours of red and green on his left paw with a big red and green bow around his neck. There was also a 'Cheeky' available to buy in the same design.

Novelty items sell well at Christmas and much like the Steiff factory, Merrythought have also produced some wonderful hanging Christmas tree ornaments over the years. The ones that I think are the most fun are those which show a 'Cheeky' bear head and arms poking out of a round ball which forms their bodies. Each of the balls has the year embroidered on it and they are hung on the tree branches with ribbon. Available in rich reds and deep greens these decorations would brighten up any Christmas tree.

FACT
Merrythought's name is derived from the old English word for a wishbone. A symbol of good luck Merrythought registered the wishbone as its logo in 1930.

HERMANN BEARS

Johann Hermann, a toy maker from the village of Neufang, Germany, persuaded his family to join him in making teddy bears. Five years later in 1912 Johann's eldest son, Bernhard, decided he wanted to set up his own company with his wife Ida so they left the family business, moved to Sonneberg and set up their own bear making company, under the trademark BE-HA.

With the help of Ida, his four sons, and a small amount of employees, Bernhard started to see his company grow. After World War Two Sonneberg found itself under Soviet rule so Bernard relocated his family and business to Bavaria. It was here he changed the company name to Teddy-Pluschspielwarenfabrik, Gebruder Hermann KG, which when translated reads Teddy Plush Toy Factory, Gebruder Hermann KG. The Germans shorten this and know the bear making company as Teddy-Hermann. It was also at this time that the trademark was changed to read HERMAN teddy ORIGINAL which is found on the famous red seal that every bear wears.

Hermann bears are of the highest standard. All are hand stuffed using a funnel, have hand-stitched noses and are made with the finest quality mohair and woven materials. They have also produced ranges of Christmas bears over the years and many bear tree ornaments like the 2002 'Sugar Plum Fairy' and 2003 'Poinsettia' teddy hanging tree decoration.

ARTIST BEARS

Right around the world there are thousands of talented and skilled makers of teddy bears. The majority of these being relatively small companies or even sole traders and are referred to as makers of artist's bears. For me some of the most delightful bears are made by these numerous companies and it is important when collecting them that you take into consideration, the time, effort and talents that make each of these little teddies. Some artist bear companies are very commercially viable whilst others aren't as well known but all of these bears are worth purchasing as they are made with heart and passion. I tend to support my local bear makers and 'Holly' a Christmas bear that I recently found was made by Billybob Collector's Bears, which operates in my local area of Essex. Again many produce Christmas inspired bears and it is worth buying them because they are all handmade, with many being one-off designs, so no other collector will be able to buy the same bear, making yours unique.

This sweet little artist bear is called 'Holly' and was made by one of my local bear artists Billybob.

Caring for your Bear

Greatly loved by their owners, bears need to be looked after and taken care of so here are some tips on making sure your bear leads a long and happy life.

- Keep your 'hug' away from moths and bugs – place a UV light near your bears as this will deter horrible bear eating creatures.
- If nasties do get at your treasured bear then place him in a polythene bag with moth-balls.
- Display your bears in a dry atmosphere away from direct sunlight or changing temperatures.
- If you need to wash your bear wipe him down with a damp cloth.
- Never place him in the tumble dryer!

CHRISTMAS BEAR COLLECTING

If you decide that a Christmas bear is for you than make sure that you choose carefully as there are thousands to choose from and all have their own special features. Smaller limited edition sizes are advisable or those that have sell out success in the shops. Quality always stands the test of time and the more innovative the better so look at those that have unusual qualities. However, the most important tip is to make sure you buy a bear that 'speaks to you' as this is sure to put a smile on your face every time you hug him.

CHAPTER 16

A BOARD CHRISTMAS

A long-standing tradition in my family is to sit around the table on Christmas night with the latest board game. I remember playing all the old favourites like Cluedo, Ludo, and the horse racing game Escado. However, my family also always wanted to sit down to a game of Monopoly – my least favourite – as I never ever won.

Collector's Tips
Look for board games dating to the Victorian era, especially those made by McLoughlin as these are rare and desired collector's pieces. One of the rarest McLoughlin being 'Bulls and Bears' which can be worth as much as £5,000 to £6,000

A long-standing tradition in my family is to play board games at Christmas and there are many rare and sought after vintage ones to find.

Monopoly was first produced in America in 1936 by Parker Brothers; in the same year John Waddington obtained the licence to have the game published in the United Kingdom. However, the history of the game dates back even further as Lizzie Magie, a Quaker from America, invented and patented a very similar board game 'The Landlords Game' in 1904. It is believed that some years later an unemployed salesman, Charles Darrow came across Lizzie's game and decided to have a go at making his own. The game proved popular with his family and friends so Darrow began to make more and sell them for a few dollars each. Department stores were soon taking the game and before Darrow knew what was happening the orders rapidly increased. Darrow then approached Parker Brothers to see if they would take the game, but they declined, so Darrow hired someone to help him make 5,000 to fulfil the department store orders he had. By chance the president of Parker Brothers came across the game when a friend purchased it and he immediately contacted Darrow and offered to buy the game and give all the royalties to Darrow. Charles Darrow was soon to become a millionaire and the first inventor of a game to make that much money.

Collecting Monopoly boards is quite complex as the board was made of various materials, the box was produced in different colours, and even the pieces and money varied. However, the original Darrow games are extremely rare and if the board is made with oilcloth and measures to twenty inches you are looking at the first ever monopoly game made in 1934. The Darrow white box is also the rarest box to find and the money from this first edition had the amount in the centre only, rather than later issues which additionally show the monetary value in all four corners. Dice can also help identify the games age as the original first edition was made with a silver metal hollow die, the second edition die was made of bone and later issues, after the Parker Brothers trademark was set on the game in the 1940s, usually have a white Bakelite die, although sometimes it can be green or red Bakelite and very occasionally wooden.

Still one of the leading board games played on a daily basis, Monopoly is played all around the world.

Monopoly is still one of the leading board games played on a daily basis right around the world. However, aside from the traditional Monopoly game there are now many variations to Darrow's original design. Most of those inspired by Christmas can only be found in the United States, like the collector's edition 'Rudolph the Red Nosed Reindeer', and seasonal releases 'Twas the Night before Christmas', and 'A Christmas Story' based on the classic movie.

Trivial Pursuit

One of my all-time favourite board games that I love to play over Christmas is the game that tests your ability and knowledge, Trivial Pursuit. Since its introduction in 1981 this board game has been phenomenally successful. Originally invented by two Canadians, Chris Haney and Scott Abbott, they came up with the idea in 1979 whilst playing a game of Scrabble. Initially only 1,100 games were published in Canada and these were all sold at a loss due to high production costs and the rate with which retail outlets would buy the game. Hanley and Scott had also taken on two business partners, and sold five percent of their shares to an eighteen-year-old artist, Michael Wurstlin, who helped design the artwork for the game.

By 1982 they had found a games manufacturer and distributor who worked heavily on a PR campaign and in 1984 over 20 million games were sold, ensuring Trivial Pursuit became a household name.

The perfect after dinner entertainment Trivial Pursuit has produced dozens of varied themed questions over the years including 'Tis the Season' which contains one thousand cards to test your knowledge on Christmas trivia. So what better way to spend an evening over the seasonal holiday?

Classic Christmas Film/Television Games

Board games have also been released in conjunction with Christmas films. Some are geared towards children whilst others are for adults to play as well. The Charlie Brown Christmas board game is great fun for kids, as you take the players (the *Peanuts* gang) and help them to learn the true meaning of Christmas by decorating Charlie Brown's tree, giving gifts, and collecting candy canes. Whoever is first to actually light up the tree wins. Published by Sababa toys this game tends to sell for around £20 and as there are many collectors of Charlie Brown and Snoopy memorabilia it crosses over into this category as well as Christmas.

Another children's board game that crosses over from Christmas into film memorabilia is *The Snowman*. Reasonably easy to find, I have owned this game in the past and although collectors will only part with around £10 to £15 for it, this game is a fun Christmas pastime for children; as is ' The Nightmare before Christmas' which costs slightly more to acquire. Not your traditional idea of Christmas, the basis of the game is to steal Santa, collect points and defeat Oogie Boogie but still amusing to play.

This game is great fun for the children and as it is based on the cartoon character Charlie Brown it falls into both Christmas and character collectables.

If however it's a more sophisticated Christmas themed game that you are looking for then I suggest the delightful trivia board game based on the classic film *It's a Wonderful Life*. Simply answer the questions correctly and relive all those magic scenes from the movie.

Collector's Tip

Always check the corners of the box as if they are worn or damaged it means the game inside is probably worn as well and thus won't be as sought after. Also make sure that the game has all its playing pieces and instruction booklet because if all the pieces aren't there the game is worthless.

COLLECTING BOARD GAMES

All kinds of board games are considered collectable and it is usually the more modern ones that people look for as these are easier to acquire. Many collectors choose licensed games featuring cartoon, television and film characters; buying those dating from the 1970s as they are more affordable and likely to go up in value. I have personally bought some great board games at boot sales and charity shops which I paid not more than a couple of pounds for. My best buy being a 'Titanic' game dating to 1998, which I purchased for £1 and eventually sold on for £35. Another one to look out for which I have also bought in the past for £3 is 'Hero Quest'. I have seen the advanced 1992 edition of this sell for in excess of £50 but before buying this particular game make sure all the figures are unpainted and still attached to the plastic.

A Christmas Game

Christmas is very much about enjoyment and having fun, so what better way to do this than sitting down and playing a festive board game. They are great for all the family and if you choose wisely, look after all the pieces, and then store it away someplace where the box won't get damaged it will become a collectable of the future.

CHAPTER 17

CHRISTMAS BOOKS

ometimes it is nice to take some quiet time during the otherwise frantic festive season. So if I am not decorating the tree or rushing around buying gifts I like to sit down with a good book and read for a while.

There has been a wealth of different books dedicated to the various characters and yuletide festivities we associate with Christmas. Some of these books have even been

There are a wealth of different books dedicated to Christmas, some of which are either collectable in their own right or have sparked a series of collectable items.

responsible for creating collecting phenomena such as Raymond Brigg's *The Snowman* and his *Father Christmas* series. Others simply retell enchanting stories based around the Christmas period like the *Mr Man* book *Mr Christmas*. However some books have played a major part in the way we celebrate Christmas today, with the most influential author being Charles Dickens as his series of five Christmas books re-ignited the joy of the festive season within the hearts of the Victorian people.

A Christmas Carol

A Christmas Carol was first published on 19 December 1843. It contained illustrations by the English artist John Leech and was the first of five Christmas books written by Dickens. This book is said to have been responsible for reviving the importance of Christmas, as it made the celebrating of this festive season popular again.

The Chimes

This book was written whilst Dickens was living in Genoa, Italy and was published in 1844. Very similar to that of *A Christmas Carol*, this book is concerned with a ticket porter, Trotty Veck whose life is transformed by the spirits of the chimes of New Year's Eve.

The Cricket on the Hearth

In 1845 Dickens' *The Cricket on the Hearth* was published. This is a story about a cricket that constantly chirps from John Peerybingle's hearth and acts as a guardian angel to him and his family. Very much along the same lines of *A Christmas Carol* the story ends with the miser of the book, Mr Tackleton, having a change of heart and thus a happy ending for everyone concerned.

The Battle of Life

The least popular of the Christmas books written by Dickens and published in 1846 was the *Battle of Life*. It is also the only Christmas book not to contain a ghost or phantom although he still has the running theme of a change of heart.

The Haunted Man and the Ghost's Bargain

This is the fifth and last of Dickens' Christmas books and was released in 1848. Once again, very similar to those already written by Dickens, this book tells the story of a chemistry professor, Mr Redlaw who had terrible memories until he is visited by a phantom double of himself and is given the gift of being able to forget those memories. Mr Redlaw is then able to help others with awful memories by passing on his newly found gift.

COLLECTING DICKENS

Dickens and Christmas go hand in hand. His heartfelt stories always have a happy ending and there is generally a worthwhile lesson to be learnt. When it comes to collecting Dickens material however, you will find that the most important collection is housed at 'The Charles Dickens Museum' in London's Holborn district. His only surviving London home, where he lived for just two years (1837-1839), there is much relating to the author's life from rare editions to manuscripts and paintings to furniture.

Rare example of Charles Dickens books can still be found mainly from specialist dealers and of course can cost a considerable amount of money. When researching I discovered a first edition 1843 copy of *A Christmas Carol* on a website. Apparently to authenticate a first edition you need to make sure it has all the following factors. The book must have green endpapers, a dated blue and red title page, the Stave 1 issue plus all first state text errors. It also needs to have original brown ribbed cloth cover, with gilt title and decoration to the spine. All edges also need to be gilt. If you find that you have one of these books then you will be pleasantly surprised as it sells in the region of £17,500. I found this particular copy in the rare book room on the AbeBooks.co.uk site and when I clicked onto the price – the book had already been sold.

RAYMOND BRIGGS

Two of the most classic children's Christmas books have been written by Raymond Briggs, and both have had a huge impact on the collectors' market.

The Snowman, published in 1978, tells the story of a snowman that magically comes alive after the chimes at midnight. Together with the little boy James, who built him, they have amazing adventures.

Another of Brigg's classic Christmas stories is that of *Father Christmas*, which

Raymond Briggs' The Snowman *and* Father Christmas *books have contributed to many collecting categories including ceramic figurines.*

was published in 1973. Not your usually stereotype image, Brigg's Father Christmas is ill tempered and lives in a normal house with a dog, cat and two reindeer for company. He loves his job but has to deal with all sorts of problems as he tries to deliver the presents. When finally he succeeds, he returns home to moan about all of the presents he receives – oh, apart from the bottle of booze from Fred! Father Christmas likes a tipple in this book.

THE NIGHTMARE BEFORE CHRISTMAS

This children's book was originally an animated fantasy film released in 1993. Directed by Henry Selick and co-written by Tim Burton, the film tells the story of Jack Skellington, The Pumpkin King of Halloween Town who accidentally finds a portal opening to

Christmas Town. Overwhelmed by the feeling of Christmas Jack returns to his own world with the idea of kidnapping Santa Claus and all his elves and replace them with his own ghouls to deliver his own version of Christmas.

This film and book have become iconic and as a result there are masses of memorabilia to acquire from cookie jars to toy figures and even bags to dolls.

POP-UP BOOKS

I have a bit of a fascination with pop-up books and am the proud owner of Dean's *The Royal Punch & Judy* moveable book. Dean & Son was the first publisher to produce a moveable book on a large scale. Classed as a toy book they were also credited with inventing the use of the tab mechanism. The company advertised this new moving mechanism as 'living pictures' and my book, the Punch and Judy, is one of the earliest publications with the tabs. Dating to around 1875 this book originally cost 2/s (a big difference to the £125 that I paid) but a small price to pay for the hours of happiness I have when reading and playing with it.

Jack Skellington 'RIP' ceramic tombstone Cookie Jar.

I am lucky enough to own Dean's The Royal Punch and Judy *book as played before the Queen at Windsor Castle and the Crystal Palace.*

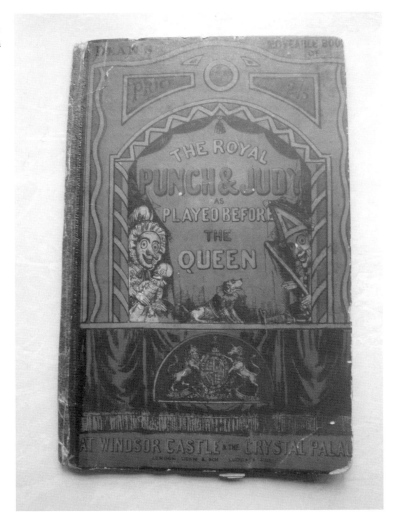

CHRISTMAS ANNUALS

You can't really talk about Christmas books without discussing the masses of Christmas annuals that are available for collectors; an integral part of children's Christmas. I remember each year receiving my *Bunty* or *Sindy* annual which would then give me hours of fun reading the stories and playing the games. Today, this is still very much a part of Christmas and each year there is a variety to buy in the shops. You can choose between iconic characters like *Beano* and *Dandy* through to football annuals and all the popular television shows such as *Dr Who* and the car programme *Top Gear* also release annuals every year.

Early annuals can command good money like the 1945 magic *Beano* comic annual which can sell for £200 to £250 or even the more recent 1998 motor racing *Le Mans* annual which

Most children receive an annual as a Christmas present, and collectors eagerly source early or rare ones.

can make upwards of £50. However, the rarest of all children's annuals has to be the 1973 brown-faced *Rupert* annual.

Mary Tourtel was the creator of *Rupert*, and her first cartoon strip appeared in the *Daily Express* on the 8 November 1920 but in 1935 the artist Alfred Bestall took over as Mary's successor.

When Alfred was presented with the 1973 annual he was not best pleased as it depicted a white-faced *Rupert* on the front as opposed to the traditional brown-faced *Rupert*. So in order to appease the artist a handful of annuals were also published with Rupert having a brown face. Today, it would be a collector's dream to find one of these rarer annuals and prices achieved in the past have been as much as £23,000 at Dukes Auction house in Dorchester, England.

BOOK BONANZA

Collecting books is a really specialised area but if, like me, you love to read this is a wonderful subject to collect. Not only do you gain enjoyment and probably learn much from reading the books, but book collecting can also be a sound investment. First editions, books signed by the author, and rare and sought after editions are highly prized. Condition is extremely important so always check for tears to book jackets, pitting and staining to pages. Make sure the spine isn't broken and if you decide to collect annuals they are more valuable if the pages are not coloured in and the games not played.

They also make affordable presents for children at Christmas, so next time you are in

The extremely scarce 1973 brown-faced Rupert *bear annual with original artwork sold at Dukes Auctioneers in 2007.*

your local book shop use your initiative to work out which of the new modern annuals will become collectable in the future. You can buy one each for the kids, and maybe try and buy an extra one to stick away and forget about for a few years, as many of the annuals are definitely winners for increasing in value in the future.

CHAPTER 18

CHRISTMAS FILM MEMORABILIA

When I am not tucked up with a good book then there is nothing more that I love than snuggling down in front of a roaring fire and watching a good old-fashioned Christmas film. In fact, I try to cram in as many of the old classics as possible because, for me, watching these movies gets me into the festive mood. Most are full of wonderful Christmas cheer with sometimes a hard luck story thrown in for good measure, but generally they always have a very happy ending, which usually ensures that I end up in floods of tears. There is also a very buoyant market for collecting film memorabilia in general and items associated with Christmas films are big business. So if the movie is a classic, or has been a blockbuster sell out success, you can guarantee there are plenty of

There is nothing more I enjoy than watching a classic Christmas film like White Christmas *and there are many Christmas collectables associated with these iconic festive movies.*

avid film buffs desperate to get their hands on the rare items of film memorabilia that can be found.

My Top Ten Christmas Films and their Collectables

Below is a list of my top ten favourite Christmas films. Most of which also tie in with Christmas collectables, as lots of merchandise has been released in conjunction with these films, one item of which made a staggering auction price. However, a couple of the films on the list do not have any collectable memorabilia attached but are just wonderful Christmas films that I feel should be part of my Christmas book.

1 – *White Christmas*

My, and possibly everyone's, favourite Christmas film has to be *White Christmas* which was released in 1954 and starred Bing Crosby, Danny Kaye, Rosemary Clooney, and Vera Allen. This wonderful story has been gracing our screens nearly every Christmas since its release and yet I still get a joyous feeling inside when I watch the perfect Christmas card scene at the end where all the heroes and heroines are adorned in Santa inspired costumes watching the snow finally fall.

Collectable memorabilia for this film goes from both ends of the spectrum. I own a special limited edition boxed video set that includes an exclusive twenty-page brochure entitled '*Remember by Rosemary Clooney*' and is only worth a couple of pounds. There are also reproduction film posters on the market and occasionally you will find an original film cell, none of which command great deals of money. However, an original 1956 film poster can sell in excess of £1,000 but the biggest collection of rare *White Christmas* memorabilia can be found at the Rosemary Clooney House museum in America. Dedicated to this amazing actress one of the prized pieces was sourced in quite an interesting way.

The blue dress worn by Clooney whilst performing the famous *Sisters* song and dance routine in *White Christmas* was bought by Kathy Brown on eBay for a measly $200 (£100). The sellers of the dress obviously weren't aware of the significance of this ensemble as they had picked it up from a vintage clothing store in California. Kathy started the complicated authentication process as soon as she had the dress in her hands. She began by blowing up still shots from the movie and went carefully through every section where Clooney had worn the dress. Kathy was able to view other costumes already on display in the Rosemary Clooney museum to compare how Paramount had sewn the seams and installed the zips. Everything matched – this bargain buy from an internet auction turned out to be the genuine article.

The dress is now on permanent display in the *White Christmas* room at the Rosemary Clooney House museum. Other artefacts in this special room include a pair of rhinestone gloves worn in a performance scene by Clooney, original movie posters and other outfits worn by the cast at parties. For me, this is the fitting place for the blue dress to reside, as it seems this simple garment has been on a real adventurous journey and now has finally come home.

2 – *It's a Wonderful Life*

A very close second in my top ten of Christmas films has to be Frank Capra's 1946 *It's a Wonderful Life* staring James Stewart and Donna Reed. The heartfelt warmth of the Christmas spirit makes the ending to this film one of the most memorable and also one of the most collectable when it comes to associated memorabilia. Avid collectors source posters, lobby cards, press books and autographs with one of the top prices achieved being for an original one-sheet 1946 movie poster which sold for a staggering $15,535.

Collector's Fact

The original 1946 movie posters and associated memorabilia are extremely rare but the film was re-released from the 1950s onwards and these posters, although collectable are not in the same league, price wise, as the originals. Foreign posters are also desirable as the film was released in various other countries. The 1948 French version which is set on a dark blue background with James Stewart depicted on the front handing out money from the bank roll scene is a real treasure if found and is worth around £300 to £600 if in really tip-top condition.

Other memorabilia to look out for from this classic movie are autographed cast photos, original film cells, and even the 1990 reissue posters, which can sell for around £30 each.

3 – *A Christmas Carol*

I am also a bit of a fan of *A Christmas Carol* and remember my little brother and me sitting huddled up on the sofa watching the really scary 1951 version starring Alistair Sim. Well actually we spent most of the time watching the film from behind the sofa, as being very young children Scrooge and the ghosts were a little frightening. However, my favourite of all the Scrooge films is the 1970 musical version with Albert Finney as it really gets you into the festive spirit – so to speak.

4 – *The Nightmare Before Christmas*

The 1993 animated Disney film, *The Nightmare Before Christmas* is the perfect antidote to an overload of festive sentimentality and has also produced masses of merchandise, much of which has become highly collectable. Aside from the usual movie posters, film cells and action figures you can also find an array of unusual items like Converse All Star trainers decorated in scenes and characters from the film. Sculptures like the rare earthenware 'I'm Mr Oogie Boogie' sculpted by Patrick Romandy-Simmons for WDCC and many action figures, as well as three-dimensional snow globes, make around £80 each.

5 – *The Snowman* by Raymond Briggs

The minute I hear the tune *Walking in the Air* I can't help but sit down in front of the television and watch the film that I associate most with children's Christmas animation. *The Snowman*, as already discussed, has made a huge impact on the collectables market with a whole catalogue of various products and merchandise available to buy. Depending on what you want to collect you can choose between items including ceramic figurines, board games, plush toys, pin badges and stamps: a great subject matter for children to collect or adults that are driven by nostalgia.

6 – *Frosty the Snowman*

A real child at heart, I love all the kid's films and the television thirty-minute animated

Tim Burton's The Nightmare Before Christmas *film has heaps of associated memorabilia including many toy action figures.*

film *Frosty the Snowman* is definitely on my top ten list of Christmas entertainment. Released in 1969 this short animation film tells the story of a discarded silk top hat which magically brings a snowman to life. This then ends up in a struggle between a group of children and a magician who wants to steal the hat. Realising that Frosty will melt unless he finds colder climates, together with a friend, Frosty stows away on a train headed for the North Pole. Does he melt? Will the Magician steal his hat? Well you will just have to watch to find out . . .

In 2003 Royal Doulton issued a series of ceramic ornaments which are often referred to as 'Frosty the Snowman' although the official title for the range was 'Frosty Family'. There have also been a few Christmas plates entitled 'Frosty the Snowman' such as the one released by Bing & Grondahl in 2003 which was the 109th plate in their Christmas series.

7 - *Miracle on 34th Street*

This film questions, 'Is there a real Santa Claus?' It is about a man who claims to be Kris Kringle, more widely familiar as Santa Claus, but no one believes him. So he spends his entire time trying to prove his identity. This movie can be seen every year on television and is another that sets the Christmas mood.

8 - *How The Grinch Stole Christmas*

This film, based on the classic 1957 book by Dr Zeuss, stars Jim Carrey as the Grinch, a strange green man who lives in the mountains outside the town of Whoville. A bitter creature with a heart 'two sizes too small' he hates Christmas and tries to do anything he can to ruin it for the Whovillians, so he steals their food, toys and decorations. This obviously doesn't stop Christmas from coming so he soon realises that Christmas is much bigger than decorations and presents. He returns everything he stole and his heart grows three sizes larger enabling the Grinch to join the town's folk and learn the true meaning of Christmas.

Whilst writing this book much of the props from the original film were being sold on an internet auction. They included Jim Carrey's Grinch green nose and a pair of his furry shoes with full authenticity documentation. When buying anything associated with a specific person, film or event what we call in the trade 'provenance' is really important to obtain. This generally is in the form of a paper trail and proves that the item did belong to that person in question. If you can authenticate the piece this adds so much more value.

9 - *The Muppets Christmas Carol*

A Muppet Twenty-fifth Anniversary Corgi car with Fozzie Bear at the wheel, in original box.

I know, but I like the Muppets, they make me laugh and this adaptation of Dickens' classic story is fun. Although there is not much in the way of Christmas Muppet memorabilia there are collectors who amass items associated with the strange collection of Muppet characters. The two leading stars, Kermit and Miss Piggy, generally draw the biggest attention and a vintage bendy 1977 Miss Piggy toy makes around £80, whilst a collection of four original Muppet Corgi cars dating to the late 1970s command £75 or more, as opposed to the later twenty-fifth anniversary models which make half this price. So not really Christmas collectables but definitely an iconic vintage television show which has a faithful following of collectors.

Fact
In 1979 Pelham Puppets released the marionettes of Kermit and Animal. They also created prototypes for Miss Piggy and Rowlf the Dog but these two were never put into production.

10 – *The Wizard of Oz*

Ok, so not a typical Christmas themed film but certainly one that gets aired every seasonal period. This wonderful story of Dorothy, her red shoes and her journey through the Land of Oz is a classic film, which has produced some fantastic collectables. The record auction price held is for a pair of Judy Garland's ruby red slippers, one of several pairs made for the film: they sold for a staggering £345,000 at Christies in 2000. Most people though, would never be able to afford this particular piece of memorabilia but there are still many associated products on the market. Royal Doulton issued a limited edition set of *The Wizard of*

Madame Alexander full set of The Wizard of Oz *dolls which were given away with McDonalds in America.*

Oz figures in 1999 to commemorate the films sixtieth anniversary which today sell for around £350. There have also been a variety of dolls such as the Barbie talking 'Dorothy' and the Madame Alexander dolls given away as freebies with McDonalds in the United States.

THE END . . .

I love to watch these films over and over again. Not only because the heartfelt stories place me in a happier more festive mood but also because each and every one brings back memories of Christmas past. One of the reasons I am so passionate about collecting is the social history that goes with each and every item. These films are very much a part of our film and social history and so the abundance of associated collectables are also helping to keep the nostalgia alive.

CHAPTER 19

A SPARKLING CHRISTMAS

Being a bit of a shopaholic one of the most exciting things that I love during the run up to Christmas is buying my Christmas outfit, shoes and handbag. It is important as a girl that you get these things just right and as soon as I have decided the next important decision is what jewellery to wear with it. The most important for me when buying jewels is that I buy something that not only looks fantastic but is also classed as a collectable. Aside for the general things that you can purchase in the shops there are many wonderful items that can be found in collectable centres, vintage stores and even on internet auctions. The trouble is with so much to choose I end up going a little over the top and buying more than I need. However, this works in my favour because I then end up giving surplus items away to friends as their Christmas presents. So what is there out there to buy that not only looks amazing but also has a Christmas collectable following?

BEDAZZLING COSTUME JEWELS

Some say diamonds are a girl's best friend but in my case it's not diamonds that make me sparkle but the wonderful array of non-precious metal costume jewels that can be found. Even though for centuries people have adorned themselves with decorative artefacts the customary wearing of a Christmas corsage only dates back to the late Nineteenth Century. Originally made from material such as ribbon not many have survived as they only lasted a few years but by the early to middle Twentieth Century more durable materials were available enabling manufacturers to produce a host of different designs in jewellery for Christmas.

The thing I love about costume jewellery is that it is far more innovative and unusual in design than the fine precious jewellery and you can also choose to invest at any price. The other significant factor is that you can either buy into certain designers or choose to collect themes. Then there is, of course, the extra bonus that you will probably never find anyone else wearing the same piece as you – making your Christmas jewellery unique and ensuring that you stand out in a crowd.

I own a stunning Butler & Wilson necklace which reminds me of coloured Christmas tree baubles.

CHRISTMAS JEWELLERY; NAMES TO CONJURE WITH

So when it comes to collecting costume jewellery or simply buying a nice piece to complement your Christmas day outfit, where do you start? I think you first need to consider whether you want to look at vintage pieces or prefer to stick to contemporary designs. I have a bit of both but that's because I am obsessed with jewellery buying. As with anything, I purchase what attracts my eye so my small collection consists of a very modern Butler & Wilson necklace to a vintage 1950s Matisse copper necklace. It really is down to what suits your personal taste and there are many different vintage and modern designers to choose from: here is a list that might give you some guidance.

- Butler & Wilson
- Chanel
- Christian Dior
- Cristobal
- Eisenberg
- Erickson Beamont
- Hollycraft
- Joseff of Hollywood
- Lea Stein
- Lulu Guinness
- Marni
- Matisee/Renoir
- Miriam Haskell
- Sarah Coventry
- Schiaparelli
- Stanley Hagler

- Swarovski
- Tom Binns
- Trifari
- Vivienne Westwood

CHRISTMAS TREE PINS

One of the most exciting areas of Christmas jewellery collectables is that of Christmas tree pins. These ornate pins really became popular during the 1950s when American servicemen fighting in the Korean War were sent them by their families and loved ones. Very much in tune with Christmas these pins are made of gold tone, gilt and metal and feature rhinestones, beads and generally much enamelling. Many of the costume designers of the time produced these pins and even today they are still being made ensuring that there is a solid collectors' market for both the vintage and the modern examples.

CRISTOBAL

The British company Cristobal was founded in 1986 specialising in making contemporary jewellery with a vintage feel. Using only high quality Austrian crystal, which generally dates to the 1940s and 1950s, each piece is hand set within the design. In the 1990s the two owners Yai Thammachote and Steven Miners produced limited edition designs. These were split into four different collections with one of these being the 'X-mas Collection', which of course featured stunning Christmas tree pin brooches.

EISENBERG CHRISTMAS TREE PINS

The American clothing company Eisenberg Original started to accessorise its dresses with decorative pins during the 1930s. These pins proved so popular with their customers that it wasn't long before they were being sold separately. The designs varied and included floral as well as figural styles. Another design that Eisenberg

A sparkling Eisenberg Original Christmas tree pin brooch.

started to produce was that of Christmas tree brooches and both the vintage and modern examples are highly collected today.

> Dating an Eisenberg piece is relatively easy as those produced from the mid-1930s to 1945 are marked with Eisenberg Original or just Eisenberg, whilst the later ones after this date carry the marking Eisenberg Ice. Some pieces dating from the 1960s through to the 1990s carry no signature and are harder to date. Eisenberg is still making jewellery today.

The pins designed by Eisenberg are varied in design; some are very simplistic in form featuring frosted white enamel to give the impression of snow then decorated with coloured rhinestones. Others are more ornate on pierced gilt metal casting but all heavily feature the coloured rhinestones. Prices are also varied ranging from as little as £20 to over £100 depending on the age, design and collectability of the piece.

HOLLYCRAFT CHRISTMAS TREE PINS

Another manufacturer who is well known for producing Christmas tree pins is Hollycraft. During the 1950s Hollycraft produced a great deal of costume jewellery that was very colourful and Victorian in style. The company was in business until the mid 1970s and today their Christmas tree pins are now amongst the most sought after.

STANLEY HAGLER

One of the most renowned costume jewellery makers of the Twentieth Century, Stanley Hagler worked as a business advisor to Mariam Haskell before setting up his own company in the 1950s. His jewellery was intricate and opulent in design and he specialised in using faux pearls, which were hand-blown glass dipped into a pearl resin around fifteen times in order to obtain the luminosity that he required. He also worked extensively with Swarovski crystal and was awarded eleven times at the Swarovski awards for Great Designs in jewellery. He is also renowned for making some of the most magnificent Christmas tree pins, which were both outstanding in quality and more innovative than some of the other pins available at the time. Sadly Hagler passed away in 1996 but jewellery is still being made under the Stanley Hagler & Company name.

Spot a Stanley Hagler Christmas tree Pin

Hagler used hand-wired frames for his jewellery rather than the usual solid metal bases. He also often applied Murano glass beads to design the tree pin although occasionally he would also incorporate rhinestones to the designs.

Maker's Mark
A Stanley Hagler piece dating to the 1950s has Stanley Hagler printed across an oval disc. From 1983 when he moved to Florida the signature changes to Stanley Hagler N.Y.C. Pieces that are found with Stanley Hagler NYC with no full stops in between are those designed by Ian St Gielar who took over as chief designer and continued to make the jewellery after Hagler's death.

LEA STEIN

Lea Stein has become one of the most recognised female designers in costume jewellery. Both her earlier vintage creations and more modern offerings are eagerly sought after, as her unique distinctive designs are amongst the hottest collectables on the market and she too has produced some amazing Christmas tree pin brooches.

Born 1931 in Paris, very little is known of Lea's early life although it is rumoured that she spent much of her childhood in a concentration camp during WW2 which is where she supposedly met her husband Fernand Steinberger. However, we are aware that in the late 1950s Lea trained as an artist and set up her own textile company before her husband unearthed a process which would ensure Lea's standing as an innovative jewellery designer.

By experimenting with paper thin celluloid (rhodoid) acetate sheets, Fernand discovered that he could create a multi-layered effect that could then be incorporated with materials such as metallic, straw, lace and other textured fabrics. These were then blended and baked to harden, the result being a substance which resembled Bakelite yet was a totally unique plastic which could then be hand carved into various shapes. As with anything the initial piece, the master, has to be created first and to perfect this piece could take as long as six months. Once the original master (or component to use its official term) was just right then it could be used to produce many more pieces.

Amongst the many designs that Lea Stein

Lea Stein created a range of Christmas tree pins made of thin celluloid sheets, each was a different colour with a unique sparkling effect.

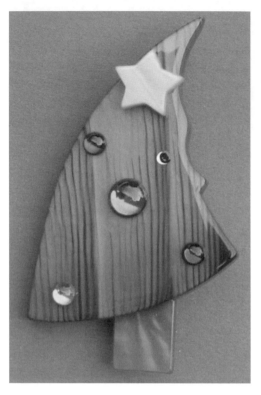

An abstract Marie-Christine Pavone Christmas tree pin applied with coloured faux gem stones.

has produced over the years are a wonderful set of Christmas tree pins. The set consists of a red/burgundy, a lavender/orchid purple, blue, white, black, light/dark green with the rarest colour being a peach/orange. Some were decorated with a lace inset whilst others had glitter to give that extra festive sparkle. This set of seven pins was available to buy in a limited edition set of just fifty which makes them very desirable to collectors.

MARIE-CHRISTINE PAVONE

Well known for her chunky, whimsical and fun jewellery designs of cats and other animals, French jewellery designer Marie-Christine Pavone has a massive following in the collectors' market. Every piece that Pavone creates is hand cut and coloured from a material called Galalith (a mixture of solidified milk casein and a small amount of formaldehyde). This material lends itself particularly well to colour and so is the perfect forum for producing fun and vibrant costume jewellery.

Aside from the many variations in cats and animals, Marie-Christine Pavone has also created some stunning Christmas tree pin designs. You can choose between a more traditional looking tree in green, which has hand painted decorative candles and baubles, or there is a range of more modernist arty trees. Each of these has an applied star at the top in yellow and coloured faux gems which give the impression of tree decorations. These trees are also not traditional in form but far more abstract looking, which I feel showcases the impressive creativity of Pavone's work.

Fact
Galalith translates as 'gala – Greek for milk' and 'lithos – Greek for stone'

TRIFARI

Gustavo Trifari was an Italian who emigrated to America to begin work with his uncle making costume jewellery. In 1910 together with his uncle he founded the company Trifari and Trifari but it wasn't long before he branched out on his own and set up Trifari. Employing a sales manager, Leo Krussman, who in 1917 brought the commercial success that he needed. He went on to employ a further sales manager, Carl Fishel in 1923, and once again changed the name to Trifari, Krussman and Fishel. In 1930 Alfred Philippe joined as chief designer and this was when the costume jewellery company really started to expand. However, in 1994 after the company had been passed down to his three sons Trifari became part of the Monet Group which in turn was bought out in 2000 by Liz Claiborne.

Trifari designed for many Broadway shows and more recently his jewellery has been seen on celebrities including Madonna when she stared in the musical film *Evita*. Over the years there has been a huge diversity in styles from floral, patriotic, and foliage to the highly sought after 'Jelly Belly' pins. Another range that Trifari produced was of Christmas tree pins and one of my most favourite is that of the 1950s 'Partridge in a Pear Tree' which shows a beautifully enamelled coloured partridge perched on the middle branches of a tree surrounded by eight gold enamelled pears. This particular design is slightly more desirable, in my opinion; and whereas a Trifari Christmas tree pin would normally sell for around £50 plus this one can make more depending on the condition.

WEISS

Albert Weiss set up his own jewellery making company after leaving employment with the Coro Company in 1942. By the 1950s and 1960s he was extremely successful to the point that much of his work was contracted out to Hollycraft so that he could keep up with the customer demand. He produced everything from bracelets to earrings and necklaces to brooches and each was made to the highest quality. Like other companies he used Austrian crystals but his were exceptional and when applied to the designs it ensured that his jewellery really stood out. Mainly flowers, fruit, foliage and figural, Weiss also designed some of the most stunning Christmas tree pins which today are classed as prized pieces.

Other Christmas tree designers and manufacturers to look out for are:

Attwood & Sawyer – Horace Atwood founded his jewellery company in Britain in 1956. Much of their jewellery was copied from Eighteenth and Nineteenth Century styles and they provided pieces for big American TV shows like *Dynasty* and *Dallas*. They produced some of the best Christmas jewellery which included tree pins as well as other festive characters.

Avon – Avon first started adding jewellery to their line of products in the late 1920s. Amongst their many lines of affordable jewellery are much Christmas inspired items

A much stylised JJ Christmas tree pin brooch in gold tone with faux jewels.

such as snowman earrings, enamel pin brooches, and of course a selection of Christmas tree pins.

Butler & Wilson – Nicky Butler and Simon Wilson opened a shop in London during the early 1970s to sell their jewellery designs. Today they are one of the most sought after contemporary jewellers with shops all over the world. Their style is contemporary based on vintage looks and happens to be one of my most favourite of all jewellery makers.

JJ – Jonette Jewellery produced lovely gold tone Christmas tree pins. They closed during World War Two although Jonette carried on making jewellery until 2006.

Larry Vrba – Larry Vrba worked as chief designer for Miriam Haskell before working on his own career. Vrba designs are extremely theatrical and over-the-top.

Mylu – The Mylu Design Company ceased trading in the 1970s. They manufactured many novelty and figural pin brooches in gold plated metals decorated with rhinestones and enamel work.

Sphinx – A British design house established in 1947 and which specialised in costume

Unsigned Christmas tree pins are also desirable with collectors and come in a range of different designs.

jewellery. Sphinx was at its height in the 1950s when it produced pins for ladies to wear on their lapels.

UNSIGNED CHRISTMAS TREE PINS

Although many collectors of costume jewellery tend to home in on those signed by prestigious makers many pieces can be found not bearing a signature. This is also true with Christmas tree pin brooches but it does not necessarily detract the value. Many of the unsigned pieces are still highly desirable and most of these date to the 1950s, meaning that they are still vintage pieces. Once again depending on style, condition, and whether the brooch is enamelled or bearing rhinestones, determines its collectability but most collectors of these pins want to acquire as many designs as possible and are willing to pay from £25 or more for the unsigned examples.

OTHER CHRISTMAS PIN BROOCHES

Even though it is the Christmas tree pin brooches that have a strong following many of the companies previously mentioned also produced other Christmas inspired costume jewellery. The brooches came in various forms such as snowmen, Christmas bells, wreaths and angels. Another popular pin is that of the poinsettia flower which is also associated with this time of year. One of the most sought after poinsettia brooches was designed by Alfred Philippe for Trifari. A rich red colour the brooch was decorated with faux rubies and diamonds and if you manage to find one of these today it would set you back a staggering £500 to £700.

ALTERNATIVE CHRISTMAS JEWELLERY

One of my favourite pieces of modern costume jewellery that I own is a stunning multi-coloured pearl cluster necklace by Butler & Wilson. A very heavy piece it looks very much like Christmas baubles and although I don't think it was made as a Christmas piece it certainly has the look. A snip at £58, I believe that this necklace is a definite investment for the future.

In fact all of the Butler & Wilson costume jewellery ranges could easily fit into the category of collecting Christmas jewellery as the stunning pin brooches, necklaces, earrings and bracelets all have the sparkle and bling that fits so well into this festive season. They also produce pieces in vibrant reds, greens, gold and silver and each one is either covered in Swarovski crystal, which sparkles like diamonds, or has wonderful faux gems.

However, if it is specific Christmas pieces you are looking for Butler & Wilson can also supply as they have made a range of comical reindeer pin brooches. One is entitled

'Dancing Reindeer' which shows three in a cancan dance pose, and another is of three reindeers all wearing their Christmas jumpers. You can also find enamelled snowmen, angels and a very bling crystal Father Christmas, as well as an earring set which looks like angels' wings.

AN AVON CHRISTMAS

Another company that produces more affordable but very festive Christmas costume jewellery is Avon. Aside from their make-up, perfumes and other beauty products there is generally a nice selection of earrings, necklaces and brooches either in Christmas character form such as Santa and angels, or more glitzy Christmas pieces, all of which would be a dazzling complement to any Christmas outfit.

Butler & Wilson are still producing Christmas tree pins today which are covered in Swarovski crystals and faux gems amongst a wonderful array of bling Christmas jewellery.

A CHARMED CHRISTMAS

If it isn't necessarily the razzle-dazzle of a vibrant Christmas but a more contemporary jewellery design that you are looking for then there are many high-end specialist jewellery makers that can provide. Recent years have seen the return of the charm bracelet as a major fashion icon and one of the most collected at the moment is the sweetie bracelet by Links of London. Releasing and discontinuing charms at regular intervals has made it quite difficult to find those that are no longer in production. At Christmas they cash in by bringing out festive charms and these are always popular. One of my favourites being the 'Christmas Bells' charm released in 2008. There has also been a candy cane, reindeer and jingling bell silver charm – all of which look stunning on a bracelet or even hooked onto a necklace as a pendant.

Tiffany & Co. is another name synonymous with both jewellery and the collecting market. If you are looking for something that little bit special this well known jeweller has something to offer – although these are more in the league of those who have a pretty penny to spend. The Christmas tree charms available through Tiffany's are of the most exquisite, made from 18k gold, the cheapest with multi-coloured gemstones is priced at £1,050. However, if you find platinum more desirable then the stunning tree charm with diamonds, onyx, tsavorites and pink sapphires will set you back an amazing £1,325 (without a chain). These pieces are obviously for those collectors where money is no object but what a fantastic item to add to your Christmas jewellery collection.

VINTAGE CHARMS

If you prefer vintage jewellery to modern then there are a host of different Christmas charms out there that can be found. The majority are made of gold and you have to hunt internet auctions, antiques fairs and specialist antique jewellery shops but there are lovely ones to be found such as angels, reindeers and Father Christmas. These are also far more unique than those available from the modern jewellers thus adding even more appeal to your collection.

ALL GEMMED UP

Although there is much to choose from in collectable Christmas jewellery I tend to go for good established names and innovative designs. Each year you can pick up cheaper options like flashing Santa earrings or over the top tacky brooches but it is far more appealing to wear something that either has some age or alternatively is a well-designed piece of jewellery as these pieces will ultimately stand the test of time. I also adore a bit of bling and as the holiday season is all about glitz I tend to home in on those pieces that sparkle. Once again buying jewellery is down to personal taste but before you start shopping make a decision as to whether to go vintage or modern and who your favourite designs are by. Christmas jewellery is a sound investment and a great fun way of spoiling yourself so be sure to make the right decision.

Chapter 20

CHRISTMAS ACCESSORIES

We have taken a look at the wonderful costume jewellery that is available for collectors but what about all the other accessories that us girlies just love to own. One of my most favourite areas of collecting, I adore everything that falls into the vanity and fashion categories such as powder compacts, perfume bottles and of course my favourite – handbags. There is a collector's market for each of these subject matters so I feel it is important to include them within this book as many do fit neatly into the area of Christmas collectables.

HANDBAGS

Anyone that knows me will confirm that I am a self-confessed handbag addict. My collecting incorporates vintage as well as modern and the more innovative and unusual the design the better. Most collectors tend to source examples from the late Nineteenth Century onwards as very early examples of bags are rarely found, with the majority on display in museums. Originally made of animal skins these bags were used for the practical purpose of carrying food and flints, but today bags are the fashionable accessory to own especially if you are able to get your hands on the 'it' bag of the time as this turns the humble bag into a status symbol.

CHRISTMAS BAGS

There are many bags that have been produced with a Christmas theme in mind, some show images of Christmas scenes whilst others are just very sparkly and glamorous. The festive period is all about bling and glitz meaning there is an assortment of bags and purses out there that fit nicely with this time of year.

In my opinion, when it comes to contemporary handbag design, British designer Lulu Guinness is streets ahead of all the others. Heavily influenced by vintage styles, she incorporates a contemporary look with the result being an innovative work of art. Releasing both Spring/Summer and Autumn/Winter collections each year, she also produces a

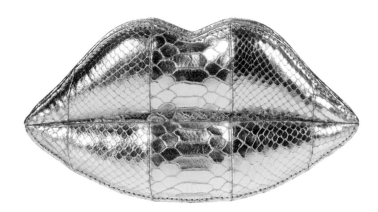

Classed by many as one of the most innovative of British handbag designs Lulu Guinness creates stunning accessories like this 'red lurex lips' clutch bag, which would complement any Christmas outfit.

'Holiday Resort' range annually. However the bags that always catch the eye of the collector are those specifically made for this market and Lulu's limited edition collector's bags are a must for any handbag enthusiast. Each of these is produced in a small limited edition production run and every design is totally unique and innovative in style. Lulu Guinness is the epitome of glamour, and her bags are highly sought after by collectors all around the world.

One bag that instantly springs to mind when thinking of Christmas is the silver 'Fairy Wing' handbag released by Lulu Guinness a few years ago. Although it was entitled 'Fairy Wings' to me it also means angel wings and has a distinct Christmas feel as it is made of shimmering silvery suede. Other bags that have the appeal of not only being highly sought after collectables but also desirable Christmas bags are the Lulu Guinness lip purse ranges. The 'Red Lurex Lips' and 'Silver Snake-skin Lips' would complement any Christmas outfit, making you the belle of the ball at the office party.

TIP
If you can't afford a designer Christmas handbag then why not look at jazzing up a cheaper bag with the Christmas bag charms that are available to buy for a few pounds.

Butler & Wilson have also produced some of the most stunning designs in handbags which although aren't instantly recognisable as Christmas collectables, do possess the desired glitz and glamour for this party season.

The Swarovski crystal heart-shaped hard clutch bag would certainly liven up a Christmas outfit as the vibrant red colour ties in nicely with festive colours. Whereas, the more subtle salmon coloured square hard clutch strikes more a picture of elegance.

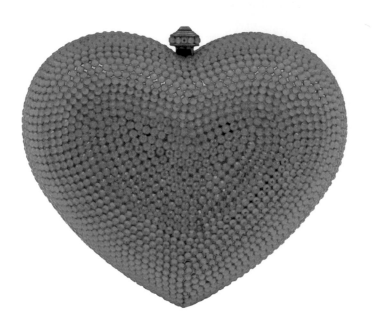

A Butler & Wilson sparking red heart clutch bag.

JUDITH LEIBER

One of the most innovative and unusual handbag designers is Judith Leiber. Her designs are completely unique and totally exquisite and if bling really is your thing then the 'Cupcake' bag is good enough to eat. Detailed with multi-coloured hand glued Austrian crystals this amazing bag would set you back a staggering $4395 but if I had the money it would be worth every penny. If however, you are looking for something with more of a wintry feel for the festive season then Judith has also designed a uniquely shaped 'Polar Bear' evening bag. Again all the Austrian crystals have been applied by hand and this bag is slightly cheaper at $3,995. The ultimate in innovative handbag design, if you can afford one buy one as Judith Leiber's designs are the ultimate prize in handbag collecting. However, if they are a little out of your price range then the answer is simple – get someone else to buy you one as a Christmas present.

Handbag Facts

- The term "handbag" first came into use in the early 1900s and generally referred to hand-held luggage bags usually carried by men.
- A shortage of leather after World War Two forced manufacturers to use cane handles.
- The Bolide Bag in 1923 was the first bag in history to feature a zipper.
- One of the most desirable and finest of handbags is the Birken made by Hermes. In

2004 a black crocodile Hermes went under the auctioneers hammer at Doyle New York for a staggering $64,800.

* The discovery of King Tutankhamun's tomb in 1992 inspired Egyptian art on handbags.

PERFUME BOTTLES

Collecting novelty commercial perfume bottles again has a massive following. Many favour vintage designs dating from the 1920s onwards whilst others concentrate on the more modern innovative bottles that are available from perfumeries and department stores. However the manufacturer I instantly think of when looking for Christmas inspired bottles is Avon. Over the years this company has released some fantastic Christmas inspired perfume bottles in a variety of shapes and sizes. Look out for those in the shape of angels, Christmas candles, bells and Christmas stockings with some being produced in coloured glass, which again are the Christmas colours of green and red whilst others are clear glass with frosted decoration. Very affordable to buy from internet auctions and collectors' centres, the Avon Christmas bottles range start from as little as a few pounds.

LADIES' COMPACTS

Powder compacts come in all shapes and sizes, some depicting historical events, others epitomising the eras in which they were manufactured. Although completely individual in design all have the same purpose – to hold those vital cosmetics that us ladies cannot live without. Over the years there have been various designs inspired which have featured Christmas imagery and these are certainly worth purchasing as they not only make wonderful gifts but also become very collectable extremely quickly.

Estée Lauder is well known in collecting circles for releasing special limited edition compacts. Many of these are available around the Christmas period and are only found in certain retail outlets. These stunning and innovative compacts come in an array of different shapes and sizes from patriotic designs to enamelled animals and even miniature coffee cups. However, one that instantly stands out as being associated with Christmas is that of the 'Snowflake' compact, this particular design is decorated in white enamel and has encrusted crystals embedded into the top. Another which is a must for any compact collector is the 2002 'Frosted Igloo' solid perfume compact as this stunning compact is covered in silver stones and a more recent release is the gold tone star compact tree ornament available in 2008.

Fact

Right up until the early part of the Twentieth Century a woman wearing make-up was often referred to as 'immoral' or 'a lady of the night'. Fortunately all this was to change in the 1920s when adornment became far more acceptable especially with the glamorous silver screen stars setting the fashion trends and influencing females to follow.

VICCI COMPACTS

The Vicci range of ladies powder compacts made by Dulwich Designs all feature wonderful art deco influenced imagery. One in particular 'Le Chapeau Blanc' has the picture of a 1920s lady on the lid wearing a big white fur trimmed red coat. This image instantly reminds me of Christmas, as she looks all dressed up in the festive colours ready to brave the winter.

STRATTON COMPACTS

The most famous British maker of powder compacts is the company Stratton; originally founded in 1860 it is responsible for a vast amount of the compacts available to collectors. Stratton was extremely innovative in its design using every image you could imagine to adorn the compacts. They also took an interest in the working mechanisms behind

'Le Chapeau Blanc' ladies powder compact from the Vicci range by Dulwich Designs reminds me of a cold winter's morning.

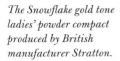

The Snowflake gold tone ladies' powder compact produced by British manufacturer Stratton.

compacts. The self-opening lid was an innovative invention by Stratton and alerted buyers to the fact that Stratton compacts prevented ladies' nails being damaged when opening it. By the 1960s Stratton's vanity items became so popular that there were agents selling all over the world. Unfortunately compacts fell out of fashion during the 1980s and the company was sold in the late 1990s.

Today, Stratton still produces some of the finest powder compacts. Many collectors seek vintage examples but there are also those that add to their collection with the more modern designs. One that instantly appeals to me, as a Christmas inspired compact, is the gold tone 'Snowflake' which has also appeared as a white enamel snowflake design. There has also been a more modern compact by Stratton entitled 'Angel' and again this fits nicely into Christmas inspired collectables.

Collecting Tips:

- Only buy good condition compacts and especially look out for missing enamel on the art deco ones.
- Ensure that the lid closes snugly – you don't want loose powder spilling out.
- Check musical mechanisms are working when purchasing.

- If bought with original box or pouch keep as this adds value and keeps the compact in good condition.
- Check the mirror to make sure there is no damage.

Taking care of your powder compacts

- Never wash as the water can get under the mirrors.
- Use a toothbrush to brush away surplus powder.
- Wipe surfaces with a soft cloth.
- Methylated spirits on a cotton bud is perfect for removing adhesive labels.
- As mentioned before storing in their original pouches or boxes keeps the compacts in good condition.

GIRLIE CHRISTMAS BLING

Christmas is a time for every girl to sparkle and what better way than with one of these glitzy handbags, festive compacts and seasonal perfume bottles. Not only are they all desirable collectables in their own right but also teamed up with a fantastic vintage dress by Ozzie Clarke, Vivienne Westwood or Chanel they would make the perfect accessories for any Christmas party.

CHAPTER 21

OTHER CHRISTMAS COLLECTABLES

There are so many offerings associated with Christmas that I have simply been unable to cover them all. You only have to consider the hundreds of food and drink products made in special Christmas packaging each year and the abundance of festive calendars or wonderful Christmas song sheets. In fact, I could spend the rest of my years writing a book on each Christmas subject; there is so much to cover. Rather than do this, I have put together some information on other things to look out for which will hopefully guide you in the right direction.

ADVENT CALENDARS

Even though I am of a certain age, I still get really excited about the chocolate Advent calendar. My partner and I have one each and they sit untouched (which is quite difficult as I am really quite impatient) on the mantelpiece until the first of December when we can both open a window and eat the chocolate. However, I always find it really hard to choose which ones to buy, as there are so many different designs.

The tradition of the Advent calendar started in Germany in the Nineteenth Century. Rather than little paper Advent calendars with windows that conceal chocolate, the early forms of counting down the days to Christmas were by burning an Advent candle or drawing a chalk line and marking off the days. The first printed

The Advent Calendar originated in Germany with the first printed one being created by Gerhard Langby in the Nineteenth Century. Today they come in many forms but it's the ones that hold chocolate that I love the best.

Advent was invented by the German, Gerhard Langby. As a child his mother had attached sweets to a piece of cardboard and each day he was allowed to take one sweet. His first printed calendar was based on this idea and consisted of miniature coloured pictures that would be attached to a piece of cardboard each day.

Today, Advent calendars are made in many different forms, some are wooden, others are made of ceramic and of course there are the hundreds of cardboard and paper ones that adorn shop shelves over the festive season. These are the ones that I love best, because what is the point of having the excitement of opening an Advent window each day and not finding chocolate behind it?

The Christmas Tin

Every year without fail you will find special tins which have been designed to house all those yummy Christmas sweets and biscuits. Beautiful illustrated scenes adorn these tins and nearly every Christmas theme has been used from robins to Santa and snowmen to evergreens. Well-known companies, like Huntley & Palmer or Cadbury, have manufactured some whilst others are just attractive festive tins.

There are many different tins available through the festive season decorated in Christmas themes such as this Churchill's sweet tin decorated with a wintry scene.

Huntley and Palmer

The most famous biscuit company in the world: Huntley & Palmer, since being established in 1882, have produced hundreds of tins many of which have been adorned with Christmas imagery.

Designs and shapes have varied over the years and those tins dating from the 1950s onwards are worth trying to track down. One design name that sometimes appears on the market is 'Joybells'. In 1952 to 1953 the 'Joybells' name appeared on an oval Peek Frean tin with a coaching scene on the lid and holly, ribbon and bell border on a red background. Then in 1961 it appeared again but this time on a square tin with bells and candles around the sides against a red and white striped pattern. The design name has also appeared on a 1968 square tin but this time the tin was decorated with Christmas scenes which were mainly biblical apart from Good King Wenceslas, who was put on to add variety.

Other tins to look out for are the 1960s octagonal tin illustrated with robins, a small round tin dating to 1958 decorated with poinsettia flowers, and the 1950s 'Snow babies' rectangular tin which shows Father Christmas with his reindeer and sleigh surrounded by snow babies with candles.

There are even earlier tins to find, and rare ones like the 1875 to 1880 'Christmas Party' are extremely scarce. Featuring a children's party taking place at the foot of a grand staircase this particular tin would be a prized possession for any serious collector.

Tin Collecting

Although amassing biscuit tins is one of the biggest areas of collecting there are all kinds of other manufacturers and types of tins to look out for. Cadbury have produced some wonderful Christmas chocolate tins, there have also been Christmas pudding tins some of which were produced by Huntley and Palmer and thousands of chocolate, tea and even tobacco tins to find. So this area of Christmas collecting would keep you pretty busy.

Condition Counts
Always try to find tins that have the fewest dints and scratches with the least amount of paint loss or rust corrosion because otherwise their value can be a lot less than those in fantastic condition.

Packaging

In fact, all forms of packaging are desirable especially if they are evocative of a period. So keep a watchful eye out for Christmas packaging that dates to the late Nineteenth and early

Twentieth Century. You can find literally every household item from cleaning products to sweet wrappers and food containers to vanity item boxes.

CAKE DECORATIONS

Unlike me, many people bake their own Christmas cake at home. I haven't the cooking skills or the time but really am envious of those that can. Cake decorations are a novelty item that is associated with the Christmas period and early examples are eagerly collected. Early Victorian cake decorations were generally made in Germany from tin or bisque. However these are difficult to come by so collectors tend to source those dating from the 1930s onwards. As mentioned in Snow babies (Chapter 10), these were originally produced as decorative items for cakes; as were many other miniature Christmas characters and scenes like Father Christmas, snowmen, miniature Christmas trees and tiny ceramic

A selection of vintage cake decorations.

houses. In later years the bisque and tin decorations were replaced with plastic ones, and these are even easier to pick up for just a couple of pounds each.

Christmas Song Sheets and Music Boxes

You know that Christmas is fast approaching when you start to hear all the festive songs being played in the middle of October.

Probably one of the most famous of Christmas songs has to be *White Christmas* written by Irving Berlin in 1942. The lyrics of the song struck a chord with the soldiers fighting in the Second World War and their families who were waiting for them back home. The recording of *White Christmas* by Bing Crosby with John Scott Trotter's orchestra and the Ken Darby Singers was so popular that it was later reprised in the movie called by the same name.

In 1994 a signed Berlin *White Christmas* song sheet was sold at Christies for $920. It

Halcyon Days have produced many festive music boxes which play classic carols including Hark the Herald Angels Sing.

was inscribed on the left middle section with the words 'All Good Wishes Irving Berlin' in blue ink.

It wouldn't be Christmas without the traditional carols and again these can be found in the form of song sheets. Many are wonderfully illustrated with festive themes and if the artwork epitomises a particular decade then this adds to their value.

Music boxes are also something worth looking at when it comes to collecting Christmas items. These usually play festive carols and again there are a host to choose from. Halcyon Days have produced many musical enamel boxes like 'Hark the Herald' which plays this classic carol. Then there are the more decorative Christmas music boxes, but still, for those who love music boxes, are very collectable.

CHRISTMAS PIN BADGES

Collecting pin badges is a popular pastime for some and, once again, there are many festive examples to find. Some are just lovely enamelled pins featuring bells, angels or Father Christmas but there are others that are worth hunting out. Look for the Disney enamelled 'Nightmare before Christmas' range, as these were shaped like Christmas baubles. The holiday camp, Butlins also produced pin badges and the 1967 Christmas one is worth purchasing as it is only about £10, also Guinness Christmas enamel badges are worth sourcing as collecting Guinness memorabilia is huge.

There are hundreds of various designs in festive pin badges, an area which is eagerly collected.

Buckingham Covers special 2008 Pantomime First-day stamp cover featuring Christopher Biggins.

PANTOMIME COLLECTING

I love going to the Christmas pantomime every year, I know it is supposed to be for children but I do tend to ignore this fact and go anyway. With lots of 'He's behind you' and booing it is just fantastic fun and a wonderful British Christmas tradition.

The principal boy (usually played by a girl), the goodies and baddies, and usually a well known story like *Aladdin*, *Cinderella* or *Babes in the Wood* all contribute to the pantomime shows which are held across Britain every year. So of course, there are many associated items to collect. Original posters and theatre programmes are the most popular in this field of collecting but there are other things to find.

Wade released a series of ceramic pantomime figures in 1997 with the horse being available exclusively to the Collector's Club members and there has also been a Buckingham Covers First-Day stamp featuring the show-stopping pantomime dame, Christopher Biggins (see foreword by Christopher). The cover has a full set of the Christmas 2008 stamps to celebrate the tradition of pantomime and they feature *Aladdin*'s Genie, Captain Hook and *Cinderella*'s Evil Queen. The cover itself has a big image of Biggins in full pantomime dame dress and carries a special Southampton postmark as this is where Biggins played the part of Buttons in *Cinderella* that particular year.

CHRISTMAS COVERED

So hopefully I now have Christmas pretty much wrapped up. There is so much on offer that all of you should find something which will appeal. You might decide that you would like to start amassing all those wonderful Christmas crackers or perhaps it is the Christmas jewellery that sets your collecting pulse racing. Whatever you decide I can guarantee that the festive spirit will take over and you soon will find yourself celebrating all year round as you uncover yet another Christmas collectable to add to that every growing collection.

FINAL WORDS
FROM TRACY

The first thing that I realised when I began to write this book was how much is actually involved with Christmas. I mean, I was aware of the obvious like the birth of Jesus Christ, giving of gifts and happiness to all mankind, but what I hadn't realised was just how big a category of collecting Christmas memorabilia actually was. Every day I would suddenly think of something else to add to the book, which would then take me off into a completely different direction of collecting.

Being a collectables expert, I am constantly aware of the current market trends, what to look out for, what's hot and what's not, and to tell the difference between a fake and

Christmas is a time for celebration, festive cheer and decorating the home in hundreds of Christmas collectables.

genuine article. However, it is the social history and nostalgia behind these wonderful antiques and collectables that really excites me. I love to learn how these items began, then evolved and finally made a mark on the industries and the people that were part of their inception. In my line of work I never stop learning and one of the biggest thrills for me is passing my knowledge onto others. So, I hope that you too will learn lots as you read through the pages.

Then there have been all the wonderful people that have helped me in this quest, like those members of the Golden Glow of Christmas Past organisation which is a forum of pre-1966 Christmas collectors. I hadn't even realised a collector's club like this existed. Now I know different, and was amazed when one member told me he puts up twenty-four vintage trees covered in antique and vintage ornaments every year in his home.

In fact, nearly everyone I have met during the course of writing has given great pleasure in telling me their own Christmas stories. Some reminisce on childhood Christmas memories whilst others relay humorous accounts of their Christmas Day. Then there are those that talk about all the Christmas items they remember owning which have now become highly sought after collectables and appear within the pages of this book.

So, who knows, when you next assemble that Christmas tree you might just decide that it needs a few vintage accessories or when you are shopping at your local department store you won't be able to stop yourself from buying all that collectable festive crockery and before long your home could end up a year round shrine to the seasonal period.

So that just leaves me one more thing to say and that is 'I wish you all a very Merry and Collectable Christmas'.

Tracy

ACKNOWLEDGEMENTS

There are many people that I need to thank, as each has contributed in one way or another to the writing of this book. (You know who you are.)

However my special thanks go to the following:

To my friend and fellow writer, Susan Brewer, who probably groaned every time her phone rang as she knew full well I was at the other end ready to demand yet another image. Susan, I could never have finished this book without your obsession for collecting.

Also thanks to Ann Sizemore of hometraditions, Don Black, Jerry & Darla Arnold, Kathy Martin, Alan Aldridge, David and Russell of CS Collectables, Bob Davidge, Wanda Ingham, Julie Avery and a huge thanks to Lorna Kaufman of Vectis who was a real treasure to put up with my constant stream of requests.

Huge thanks also go to my close friends Angie, Helen, Nicky and Natasha who had to put up with my Christmas stories from the middle of August! Also thanks to Su who allowed me to fill up her car in the middle of summer with all my Christmas goodies that I discovered at the boot sales.

As always, thank you mum and dad for your continued support and encouragement, even if I did snap every time you turned up for a cup of tea when I was in full flow writing the book . . .

And finally my biggest thanks go to Paul whom without his constant support I wouldn't be able to do what I love best for a living.

Directory of Specialist Dealers

Antique/Collectable Centres

Alfies Antique Market, 13-25 Church Street, Marylebone London, NW8 8DT, Email: info@alfiesantiques.com, Tel: 0207 723 6066

Grays Antique Market, 58 Davies Street, London, W1K 5AB, Tel: 0207 629 7034

Auction Houses

Dukes Auctioneers, Weymouth Avenue, Dorchester, Dorset, DT1 1QS, Tel: 01305 265080, Email: enquiries@dukes-auctions.com, www.dukes-auction.com

Henry Aldridge & Son, Unit 1 Bath Road Business Centre, Bath Road, Devizes, Wiltshire SN10 1XA, Tel: 01380 729199, Email: Andrew@henry-aldridge.co.uk, www.henry-aldridge.co.uk

Staceys Auctioneers, 959 London Road, Leigh on Sea, Essex, SS9 3LB, Tel: 01702 475614, www.staceyauction.com

Vectis Auctions Ltd, Collectable Toy Specialist, Fleck Way, Thornaby, Stockton on Tees, TS17 9JZ, Tel: 01642 570616, www.vectis.co.uk

Ceramics

Aston Pottery, Tel: 01993 852031, www.astonpottery.co.uk

C&S Collectables Direct Ltd, Victorian Business Centre, Ford Lane, Arundel, West Sussex
England, BN18 0EF, Tel : 01243 555371, , Email: enquiries@cscollectables.co.uk, www.cscollectables.co.uk

Danish Porcelain online, www.danishporcelainonline.com

Dennis Chinaworks Ltd, Shepton Beauchamp, Ilminster, Somerset, TA19 0JT, Tel:
01460 240622, Email:info@dennischinaworks.com, www.dennischinaworks.com

Direct Ceramics Ltd, 23 Boleyn Way, Hainault, Essex, IG6 2TW, Tel: 020 8500 0345,
www.directceramics.co.uk

Emma Bridgewater, Tel: 020 7371 5489, www.emmabridgewater.co.uk

Enesco Limited, www.enesco.co.uk, Tel: 01228 404022

The Chinaman, 147a High Street, Sevenoaks, Kent, TN13 1XJ, Tel: 01732 454937,
Email : lladro@thechinaman.co.uk, www.Lladro.thechinaman.co.uk

Robert Harrop Designs, Robert Harrop Designs Ltd, Coalport House, Lamledge Lane,
Shifnal, Shropshire, TF11 8SD, ENGLAND, Tel:01952 462721, Email:-
collectorsclub@robertharrop.com, www.robertharrop.co.uk, Brochure Hotline:
Freephone 0800 282354

Spode, For stockists contact, Tel: 01905 746000, www.spode.co.uk

Portmeirion, For stockists contact, www.portmeirion.co.uk

Royal Doulton, For Stockists contact, Tel: 01782 404040, www.royal-doulton.com

Tuskers, Enesco Limited, Brunthill Road, Carlisle, Cumbria, CA3 0EN, Tel: 01228 404380, Email: enquiries@tuskers.com www.tuskers.com

CHRISTMAS TREES

Hometraditions, Website: www.hometra-ditions.com, Email: Info@hometraditions.com, The Golden Glow of Christmas Past Association, www.goldenglow.org

DOLLS

Amanda Jane Dolls, P O Box 100, Lampeter, Ceredigion, SA 48 7WY, Email: enquiries@amandajanedolls.com, www.amandajanedolls.com

For further information on dolls subscribe to: The quarterly magazine, *British Doll Showcase*, Enquiries: squibbit@ukonline.co.uk, www.britishdollshowcase.co.uk

ENAMELS

Halcyon Days, 14 Brook Street, London, W1S 1BD, Tel : 0207 629 8811, Email: info@halcyondays.co.uk, www.Halcyon-days.co.uk

GLASS

Christopher Radko, www.christopherradko.com, Swarovski, Visit www.swarovski.com

JEWELLERY AND ACCESSORIES

Butler & Wilson, 189 Fulham Road, London, SW3 6JN, Tel: 020 7352 3045, www.Butlerandwilson.co.uk, Email: info@Butlerandwilson.co.uk

Cattew, www.cattew.com, Email: Julie@cattew.com, Tel: 01296 713090

Cristobal, 26 Church Street, London, NW8 8EP, Tel: 020 7724 7230,
    www.cristobal.co.uk

Decogirl, Email: wanda@decogirl.co.uk, www.decogirl.co.uk

Judith Leiber, www.judithleiber.com

Lulu Guinness, www.luluguinness.com

Ritzy, Christopher St. James, 7 The Mall, Camden Passage, Islington, London, N1 0PD,
    Tel : 020 7704 0127

STAMP COVERS

Buckingham Covers, Warrne House, Shearway Road, Folkestone, Kent, CT19 4BF, Tel:
    01303 278137, www.buckinghamcovers.com

TEDDY BEARS

Bears of Windy Hill, www.bearsofwindyhill.co.uk, Email: *info@bearsofwindyhill*
    Tel: 01274 599175

Billybob Collectors Bears, 159 The Chase,
    Rayleigh, Essex, SS6 8QS, Tel:
    01268 745713

Hermann Teddy Bears, www.herman-
    nteddy.com

Merrythought Ltd, Ironbridge, Telford,
    TF8 7NJ, Tel: 01952 433116, Email:
    contact@merrythought.co.uk,
    www.merrythought.co.uk

Steiff Teddy Bears, Bel Air, Bristol and
    West House, Post Office Road,
    Bournemouth, BH1 1BL, Tel: 01202
    555502, www.steiffteddybears.co.uk

At Christmas Laugh and make good cheer, To welcome Father Christmas

MUSEUMS

The Victoria and Albert Museum, Cromwell Road, London, SW7 2RL, Tel: 020 7942 2000, www.vam.ac.uk, V&A Museum of Childhood, Cambridge Heath Road, London, E2 9PA, Tel: 020 8983 5200, www.museumofchildhood.org.uk

FURTHER INFORMATION ON CHRISTMAS

The Christmas Archives, www.christmasarchives.com

INDEX

PHOTOGRAPH CREDITS

Amanda Jane Dolls p69

Arnold, Jerry and Darla p16, 20, 23 (upper), 24, 26, 27, 29, 32, 33, 40, 41, 42, 43, 44, 246

Ashton Pottery p156 (upper)

Billybob Bears p194

Black, Don 017, 18, 38, 45, 173, 241

Brewer, Susan p12, 36, 59, 60, 62, 64, 66, 67, 68, 72, 81, 87, 88, 94 (upper), 95, 96, 97, 99, 100, 102, 107, 110, 111, 113, 114, 128 (upper), 143 (lower), 144 (lower), 154, 157, 170, 171 (upper), 178, 181, 182, 183, 184, 185, 197, 201, 206, 212, 213, 233, 234, 245, 247

Buckingham Covers p130, 138

Butler & Wilson 216, 224, 228

C&S Collectables p76, 77, 91, 92, 124 (lower), 139, 140, 141

Carlton Ware p128 (lower)

Cattew p219, 220

Christofferson, Lars, (Danish Porcelain online) p147, 148, 151

Christopher Radko p13, 30, 46, 47, 118, 136, 222

Decogirl p223

Dennis Chinaworks p156 (lower)

Direct Ceramics p51, 80, 123, 133, 203

Dukes Auctioneers p207

Emma Bridgewater p155

Enesco p54, 56, 79, 83 (upper), 93, 131

Halcyon Days p129, 143 (upper), 237

Henry Aldridge & Sons Auctioneers p104

Lladro p75, 90 (lower), 124 (upper), 126, 127, 142, 176

Lulu Guinness p227